WOMEN SCREENWRITERS TODAY

Their Lives and Words

MARSHA McCREADIE

PRAEGER

Westport, Connecticut
London

Library of Congress Cataloging-in-Publication Data

McCreadie, Marsha, 1943–
    Women screenwriters today : their lives and words / Marsha McCreadie.
      p.   cm.
    Includes bibliographical references and index.
    ISBN 0–275–98542–3 (alk. paper)
    1. Women screenwriters—United States—Biography. 2. Motion picture
authorship—United States. I. Title.
    PN1998.2.M425 2006
    812'.54099287—dc22   2005020947

British Library Cataloguing in Publication Data is available.

Library of Congress Catalog Card Number: 2005020947
ISBN: 0–275–98542–3

First published in 2006

Praeger Publishers, 88 Post Road West, Westport, CT 06881
An imprint of Greenwood Publishing Group, Inc.
www.praeger.com

Printed in the United States of America

The paper used in this book complies with the
Permanent Paper Standard issued by the National
Information Standards Organization (Z39.48–1984).

10 9 8 7 6 5 4 3 2 1

"This morning I took out a comma and
this afternoon I put it back again."
—Oscar Wilde, on writing

Contents

CONTENTS

Acknowledgments

The lion's share of thanks goes to the women screen and television writers who were kind and flexible enough to be interviewed for this book. They did not need the press. I needed them.

The Authors Guild gave me a generous grant at a vulnerable moment, which helped me push through to the book's conclusion. As always, a group of film-friendly folks were most helpful. Some especially come to mind: Marika Lumi Morgan in Los Angeles always knew where to get insider names and info. Producer-writer Ed Zuckerman, also on the left coast, was extraordinarily generous in opening his e-mail address book filled with intelligent and open-natured women writers for television, some of whom he had hired for shows on which he was the head writer or producer. Phil Perebinosoff, then head of movies for television at ABC, was forthcoming with names, addresses, and phone numbers.

In New York City, author Jerry Vermilye never failed to inspire with his love for and knowledge of movies, and the editorial scalpel of Al Marill kept me from making a fool of myself more times than I care to remember. And I am grateful to Dan Harmon of Greenwood Press, a "line" editor with a contagious love of movies: both rarities in publishing these days, it seems.

Introduction

Writers know that the pot of gold at the end of their rainbow is in screenwriting: a tough business but lucrative and exciting if you can make it work for you. For as difficult as it has been for male screenwriters to get and keep a gig, ever since the end of World War II the movie writing business generally has been a shutout for females.

Women Screenwriters Today: Their Lives and Words aims to address and fix some of that by raising awareness of those women at the height of their screenwriting success. (And it may even give a few pointers to male film scribes, too.) It also interviews those women about their experiences in the industry, telling us in their own words how and why they write, and what drew them to writing in the first place.

At first blush it seems that this new century has been dotted with any number of intriguing, and often unique, movies by women screenwriters—and in some cases screenwriter/directors—that have made it onto the top of the heap. Some are independents, some mainstream, but they all serve to answer the questions raised in this book. For instance, how aware are women writers of the "new" women's issues, and how receptive are audiences to these selfsame issues? Do women screenwriters feel indebted, obligated, or just plain compelled to tell stories about these topics? Only the writers themselves can answer that question, but one thing is certain: these movies are good, and good in large part because of the way they have let a female consciousness and women's topics dictate their form and theme.

Under the Tuscan Sun, for example, the 2003 film written and directed by Audrey Wells, is a mainstream movie that happens to be a clever union of didacticism and popular art. This is especially apparent because in the book—a first-person travelogue by writer Frances Mayes—there were no narrative elements like Wells added: a fictive plot, an opening up of the structure. The movement toward happy independence that is the arc of the movie, even with its inevitable Hollywood-happy ending, is very different from the book, in which the writer/narrator actually does have a male partner throughout, and there is no such emotional journey. Instead, the driving force for partnership in this film, and it is not a sexual one, comes from a friend—a uniquely conceived creation—an intuitive and loyal lesbian who knows when her friend is in trouble. When they connect by telephone continents away, it's more than girl talk; it's a clever crosscutting by Wells to show us that their connection is very deep indeed.

Independent movies are an even more obvious venue for women's topics presented by female screenwriters. Filmmaker Patricia Cardoso, for instance, depending on the work of Josephina Lopez in her play and then script for *Real Women Have Curves* (2002), directed a movie with a set piece so witty and energizing it almost diminishes it to describe it in prose. In a Latina woman's update of the standard factory workers' scene, the lead, her sister, and the other workers take off their clothes and work to the rhythms of Latin music—naked—after hearing a salsa-driven diatribe about being proud of their bodies with stretch marks, cesarean section scars, and all the "curves" that real women may have.

Politically correct? Of course, and in both films. But more important, real, and fun. And with a certain urgency that seems expressly connected to a female point of view. Though why is this notable?

It shouldn't be.

In the early years of filmmaking, women screenwriters outnumbered men ten to one, with the not surprising result of some classic films, roles, and performances by and about women—many of whom wrote for, produced, requested and directed each other. Lillian and Dorothy Gish, for instance, developed their own projects, and Lillian often insisted on using writer Anita Loos, continuing a friendship and working relationship that ultimately lasted more than seven decades. (It is of course no surprise that until now, and in a patriarchal society, Gish's main creative relationship—analyzed over and over—was deemed to have been with D. W. Griffith.)

Frances Marion wrote specifically, and most successfully, for Mary Pickford. Other creative friendships and interconnections include not just the one token early feminist rediscovery, writer-director Dorothy Arzner, but also June Mathis, Clara Beranger, Alice D. G. Miller, and many others.[1]

Another cluster of intense female professional activity was formed in the war years of the 1940s. Bette Davis and Joan Crawford requested writer Catherine Turney for their films; Lenore Coffee wrote for Claudette Colbert as well as Davis and Crawford, and directors such as Lois Weber. Screenwriter Mary McCall Jr., the first woman president of the Screen Writers Guild of America, created spunky Rosie the Riveter parts for Ann Sheridan in the 1940s and also wrote (with Charles Kenyon) *A Midsummer Night's Dream*, the screen classic with James Cagney, Mickey Rooney, and many others from the Warner Bros. stock company. Frances Goodrich, who, with her partner scribe (and husband) Albert Hackett, wrote the *Thin Man* series and *It's a Wonderful Life*, helped organize the progressive wing of the Guild in the 1930s and went on to become an elected official, the Guild's Secretary. It is noteworthy that both McCall and Goodrich refused to name names during the industry's blacklisting era two decades later.

Particularly in these decades, we see women's parts that express a strong sense of self-worth, sometimes a will of iron, and characters who frequently declare and adhere to their own moral code. Think of Lenore Coffee's dialogue for *The Great Lie* (1941), capturing so well Bette Davis and Mary Astor's multilayered and constantly shifting feelings of envy, admiration, and even, ultimately, love.

Yet by the early 1950s Virginia Kellogg was the only female member of the Writers Guild. Jay Presson Allen told me that when an interviewer informed her that in the 1960s she was one of only a handful of women screenwriters, she was incredulous until looking it up and finding that indeed this was the fact.

Women Screenwriters Today: Their Lives and Words finds and interviews today's exceptions—women screenwriters who have made it—and describes their game plans. In the following chapters are tips for novice screenwriters: how to position yourself, whether it is a good idea to have a day job in the business, how to get the right agent or mentor, and what kind of work habits to have and tools to use.

Other more pragmatic issues of female bonding within the business, as well as on screen, take real life form in a movie such as *Monsoon Wedding* by writer-director Mira Nair, who picked up the script by Sabrina Dhawan, a screenwriter Nair met while teaching at Columbia Film School.

Much of this mentoring and mutual respect has born fruit. For instance, the critical and commercial success of *The Thomas Crown Affair*, a 1999 remake of the popular 1967 movie, had two progressive female parts. Rene Russo took the main one: that of a driven, professional woman in her forties who looks great, has money in the bank, enjoys an active sex life, and—ultimately—finds herself with emotions that can be touched after some protective layers have been peeled away. At last, it was said, a matching in age and intellect of romantic leads in a mainstream movie.

And screenwriter Leslie Dixon (who had successfully written women's parts for Bette Midler and Shelley Long in *Outrageous Fortune* in 1986) did another clever turn: she paid homage to Faye Dunaway, who had taken the lead in the earlier film, by creating for her the part of Thomas Crown's (Pierce Brosnan's) therapist, a very smart woman who is on to his mental tricks. And of course from the point of view of women's roles in the cinema, it is a nice part for an "older" female actor.

The Thomas Crown Affair proved that a big Hollywood film could incorporate progressive roles for women, and for professional women. Perhaps this was the best of many worlds: a successful Hollywood product; some pleasing images of accomplished women. And some reviewers pointed out that this *Thomas Crown* update also showed that a woman could write well in the detective, thriller mode.

There were other fun, exciting, and autonomous parts for women. Jane Campion brought a compelling picture of women's creativity and sexuality breaking out even in the hidebound colonial nineteenth century in *The Piano* (1993), winning an Oscar for her screenplay. Actress-writer Emma Thompson adapted and starred in *Sense and Sensibility* (1995); Susannah Grant wrote a highly acclaimed script for Julia Roberts's character in *Erin Brockovich* (2000).

Even the classics were mined, with updated spins on women characters. As the twentieth century closed, it seemed there were just not enough Jane Austen novels, with numerous versions of *Pride and Prejudice*, then *Sense and Sensibility*, *Emma*, *Persuasion*, and the edgy *Mansfield Park*. Finally, Henry James had to be enlisted for his female-centered novels: *The Portrait of a Lady* with a script by Laura Jones in 1996, and *Washington Square* by writer-director Agnieszka Holland in 1997. In a more lighthearted vein, Gurinder Chadha wrote and directed a Bollywood version of *Pride and Prejudice*, set in India, called *Bride and Prejudice* in 2005. It seemed clear that much of this "good news" was owing to the work of women screenwriters making important progress in the world of women and film.

But for a real "woman's movie" to come about, there must be more than a script. The 1994 version of *Little Women* seemed a predictive pinnacle of sorts: directed by the renowned female director Gillian Armstrong, with a script by Robin Swicord, and proactively produced by Denise DiNovi, it recalls the kind of creative collaboration among women filmmakers in the exciting, beginning years of the movie business when June Mathis, Frances Marion, Clara Beranger, and, a few years later, Lenore Coffee and Catherine Turney, all hired each other or wrote for women stars they admired or who requested them. The silent era was comparatively a golden age for women, with female screenwriters writing half of all movies copyrighted between 1911 and 1925. With Louisa May Alcott and Jane Austen on the scene once again, it would seem all is well in the world of women and film.

And how did these happy collaborations come about? And how are they forming and faring today? It does seem that a few women in the movie business finally have learned to successfully adapt that former bête noir—the old boys club—to their own ends. Molding their own projects around this matrix (rather than the female one of the earlier part of the century that until recently has been little publicized or known about), a number of women writer-directors have created their own production troupes, much as Ingmar Bergman, Martin Scorsese, and Woody Allen have done. Jane Campion, for one, chose sister countrywoman and Australian screenwriter Laura Jones for her film *An Angel at My Table* as well as for *The Portrait of a Lady*. Like another (real life) sister act, Nora and Delia Ephron, Jane and Anna Campion have written together for *Holy Smoke*; the Campions even published a fiction version of the movie, a novelization, before the film was even released.

Barbra Streisand may have been the first self-packager on the contemporary scene with her Barwood Films, but actresses such as Goldie Hawn, Bette Midler, and Jessica Lange also put together their own production and development companies in the 1980s. Michelle Pfeiffer, Nicole Kidman, Whitney Houston, and Halle Berry followed, as did Meg Ryan, Jodie Foster, and more recently Amy Brenneman, Salma Hayek, Jennifer Aniston, Drew Barrymore, and Reese Witherspoon. Other actresses like Susan Sarandon and Uma Thurman, who crave creative control, have added the role of executive producer. With at least some women at the helm wielding searchlights for good properties for women, no wonder role models—both on screen and within the industry—seem increasingly progressive.

Movies like Beth Henley's *Crimes of the Heart* (1986) that sift through feelings between sisters—that extreme metaphor for female relationships—are no longer challenged as being intriguing or even commercially viable. Other sisters, and their complicated relationships, are dramatic material in *A Thousand Acres* penned by Laura Jones in 1997, *Sweetie* (1990) scripted by Jane Campion, *The Virgin Suicides* in 1999, and the more standard comedy, *The Banger Sisters*, in 2002.

Another litmus test for women's roles, women's friendship on screen received a breakthrough response in *Julia* (1977), the film adaptation of the Lillian Hellman memoir *Pentimento* (though it did have a male screenwriter). Perhaps the genre of melodrama was the most natural setting for the push-pull of women's friendship, for movies like *The Great Lie* and *All About Eve* were still in the public's memory.

But it wasn't until the mid-1980s that a counterpart, focusing on competition that morphs into friendship, came along: *Outrageous Fortune*. It happened to be a comedy with Bette Midler and Shelley Long playing very different types thrown together in a "buddy" film, and Midler blurting out at one point that she wanted to be friends, despite or perhaps because of all their shared travails. *Thelma and Louise*, possibly because it was not a comedy, usually gets credited as the first contemporary female buddy film in 1991; it actually was not.

Another positive sign is that women who crashed into the business and toughed it out in earlier decades are still working today with terrific results. Some believe Elaine May's script for *The Birdcage* is the best of her scripts written over the last three decades, leaving aside for the moment the fascinating question whether writing for Nathan Lane's femme half of a happy gay couple is considered writing for a woman. May was nominated for an Oscar for her script for *Primary Colors* in 1999. Melissa Mathison was the scriptwriter for the box-office smash *E.T.* in 1982 (as well as the earlier *The Black Stallion*), though her authorship of the Spielberg movie only recently has become widely recognized. Mathison also wrote *Indian in the Cupboard*, *The Escape Artist*, and *Kundun*. Though people used to make much of the fact that she was until early 2004 married to Harrison Ford, this is no longer mentioned with regularity when her name comes up.

Naomi Foner (*Running on Empty, Losing Isaiah, A Dangerous Woman*), Jay Presson Allen (*The Prime of Miss Jean Brodie*, with its unforgettable line from one of her disillusioned and jealous students, "I didn't betray you. I put a stop to you"), and Anna Hamilton Phelan (*Gorillas in the Mist*) are just a few others who have consistently worked during recent decades. And almost as if to successfully demonstrate that women writers are completely within the mainstream, there are those who simply by doing it assert their right to pen a "politically incorrect" script. The versatile Amy Holden Jones, for instance, wrote *Indecent Proposal* as well as *Beethoven* and *Mystic Pizza*. Alexandra Seros, one of the few women scriptwriters to work in the action genre, has written *The Specialist* and *Point of No Return*. Kathryn Bigelow has been writer-director of *Blue Steel* and Gale Anne Hurd co-wrote *Terminator*.

Erin Brockovich (2000) provided perhaps the most compelling example of how powerful a female writer and female star can be when working together. In the introduction to the published script, Susannah Grant wrote, "I love the script I wrote. But even more, I love the movie. I love what it started as, and I love everything that was added to it by all the bright, talented people who came onto the project after me. If you get half as much enjoyment from reading it as I did from writing it, it will be time well spent." (Of course the film reflects a telling economic reality about movies in Hollywood these days: in order to get a big feature made with a big studio, a major star like Julia Roberts must be attached to the project from the getgo.)

Gurinder Chadha, who wrote and directed *Bend It like Beckham*, the

2002 movie about young women and soccer, is similarly proud of her film and of the role models it presents: "I would like girls to walk away with their heads six feet tall, chests out, grinning from ear to ear, and going, 'Wow. I can do anything.' " *Laurel Canyon*, written and directed by Lisa Cholodenko, has two cutting-edge women's roles. Kate Beckinsale plays an uptight doctoral candidate who learns to go with the flow after meeting her fiancé's mother, a hip and humane music executive played by Frances McDormand. Even Kirsten Smith and Karen McCullah Lutz's *Legally Blonde*, which seems lightweight, actually has a number of progressive roles for women: a "working girl" who gains self-esteem, a mature professor, and of course Elle (Reese Witherspoon) herself: California airhead turned top attorney.

New Zealander Philippa Boyens, who along with Fran Walsh (and Peter Jackson) wrote the *Lord of the Rings* trilogy, said she and Walsh were conscious about trying to "bring female energy" to the roles they created from Tolkien's female characters.

Openly advertised as a "chick flick," *The Divine Secrets of the Ya-Ya Sisterhood* did well at the box office and fairly well with critics in 2002. Written and directed by Callie Khouri, *Ya-Ya* fit perfectly in one critic's definition of a woman's film: concerns exclusive to women and with emotional matters at its core.[2] It was even based on a best-selling novel by a woman, Rebecca Wells. The three-generational structure includes a lifelong friendship among women and today's *de rigueur* mother-daughter strife, with Sandra Bullock as a New York playwright, Ellen Burstyn as a ditsy drama queen, and Ashley Judd as her younger version. The exemplary Maggie Smith plays a senior "Ya-Ya." To top it off, executive Bonnie Bruckheimer, head of All Girl Productions, gave the green light to the project, and Bette Midler produced it.

Of the genre scene today, Kirsten Smith says, "It seems like the chick flick got to be a larger genre. There's the female action movie and the romantic comedy and the weeper and the woman-in-jeopardy movie. The genre that we've been working in we've named the 'girl-power' genre. The female character starts without any acceptance. She spends the movie gaining that acceptance. But at the same time she's redefining the parameters of that acceptance. Erin Brockovich is a great example of that." While a new awareness of women's issues may be credited with a recasting of some of the older forms Smith lists, there *is* a new one: Girl Power. A reflection of society—in that these real life possibilities simply did not exists before—Girl Power movies, unlike romantic comedies or weeper films—are something new.

But how can writers get to the point of creating such scripts? Is it a good idea to have a day job in the business? How to get an agent or a mentor? Even . . . what kind of work habits to develop and tools to use?

"Don't be afraid to go to people in positions of power and ask for favors," advises Jane Anderson (*The Baby Dance*). Melissa Rosenberg (*The O.C.*) gives more specific advice about breaking into television writing. First, she advises, after college, go to Los Angeles. "Find a way to live, if you're not independently wealthy. Have some life experience. Know how to type. If you can, get a job as a writer's assistant so you can find out how things are done, and be on hand if something opens up. If you can't get a job as a writer's assistant—generally a hard gig to get—get a job as a literary agent's assistant. It's a brutal job that will kill your spirit. But you will form relationships with people in the business. Take scriptwriting classes at UCLA or AFI. And all the while keep writing. Then somebody may give you a shot."

A slightly different, though just as down-to-earth, plan is offered by Susan Dickes, one of the few who broke into the almost entirely male world of sitcom writing with *Just Shoot Me*, *The Drew Carey Show*, and *Mad About You*. "There are as many ways into the business as there are people working. Yet however a door is opened for you, it won't matter if you haven't got the goods," she says. "Even if you're somebody's niece or all the things they say about nepotism in Hollywood. And of course, you have to have to have your writing samples ready."

Some patterns for success do emerge. A playwright whose work is well reviewed can be catapulted to "Hollywood" sometimes with the help of an agent who gets them work. This is the case with Robin Swicord and Gina Wendkos. For Susan Emswiller, who (along with Barbara Turner, though not together) wrote the script for the award-winning *Pollock*, it was the presentation of some of her plays at a cooperative theater in Los Angeles that got her the attention of Amy Madigan, wife of Ed Harris, and eventually the request to write *Pollock*. Writers like Allison Anders sought out mentors, who happened to have been men: Wim Wenders and Martin Scorsese are among those praised. The pragmatic Amy Holden Jones, who wrote

Mystic Pizza and *Indecent Proposal*, is grateful to Roger Corman, who was the first to give her a job. A number of women screenwriters started as actresses, others as playwrights, and segued into the business. And some—mainly younger women, it seems—saw screenwriting as a career choice early and went to film school; the University of Southern California seems favored.

The writers interviewed in the following chapters also have strong, if differing, positions on screenwriting classes and gurus. "I wish I had had a mentor," laments Lisa Loomer (*Girl, Interrupted*), saying she now relies heavily on script consultant Dara Marks. Yet Gina Wendkos (*The Princess Diaries* among other films) quips, "Only lawyers take those screenwriting classes. I guess they think they can write because they do briefs all day."

Many subscribe to a three-act structure for a feature film, including Kim Peirce, who directed *Boys Don't Cry*. She traces this structure back to Aristotle. Some rely on character arcs and plot points, but others throw this out the window. Barbara Turner, for instance, said she got the scriptwriting job for *Pollock* because her pitch included the suggestion of constructing the film itself like a Pollock painting: "That is, start from the middle and work outward."

Very specific tricks of the trade are discussed. Jane Anderson finds that only a few days are needed to get the feeling for a location, but it's still important to go there, as she did for *The Positively True Adventures of the Alleged Texas Cheerleader-Murdering Mom*. Robin Swicord, by contrast, said she went to Miami for months to research *The Perez Family*, and even studied transcendental idealism in the original German to more perfectly understand her New England characters' philosophical background for *Little Women*.

Nearly all writers say they work best in the morning; some write a certain number of pages a day, no matter what.

Those who write mainstream feature films, instead of the small independent or character-driven movies, have to deal with multiple authorship and rewrites by others, a seeming inevitability in a business where the stakes are often so high that many hands are brought in to make sure a project won't fail. TV writer-producer Ed Zuckerman, who has hired quite a number of women writers for television, observes, "Television is one area of writing where you can maintain control. And it's extremely lucrative as well." Joan Tewkesbury (*Nashville*) seconds this thought, though she omitted the financial incentive. Television feature film writer Susan Rice (*Tears and Laughter: The Joan and Melissa Rivers Story*) disagrees, feeling that producers' notes alter content too much. She also fears that reality TV is taking work away from writers.

Another problem is that some writers worry about ageism, and a few have devised ways to handle these concerns. But television sitcom writers seem to accept the fact that they won't be working much after the age of 50 and plan accordingly.

It may not be practical for today's beginning woman screenwriter to think about setting up elsewhere, but in Chapter Nine, "The View from Abroad," Laura Jones, Campion, and others talk about their use of government resources for women filmmakers. They also explain how they developed contacts made in the female-friendly film industry schools of Australia and New Zealand. The French writer-director Catherine Breillat describes how a percentage of movie ticket sales automatically go to a filmmaker, a perk of French filmmaking.

The first Oscar-winning script by a woman since 1945 took nearly fifty years to arrive. Callie Khouri won for *Thelma and Louise* in 1992. Then a New Zealander, Jane Campion, for her portrait of creativity and sexuality in 1993's *The Piano*, and a Brit—Emma Thompson with her adaptation Oscar for *Sense and Sensibility* in 1995. And nine years later Sofia Coppola won an Oscar with her original script for *Lost in Translation*.

Nevertheless, new and interesting work is being done. A few women screenwriters are focusing on topics rarely, in some cases never before filmed: incest, rape, child abuse, pornography, equal pay, sexual harassment, the plight of single mothers, gender/power relations, eating disorders, coming out, lesbian friendships, and sexual harassment. Allison Anders's *Things Behind the Sun* is about her own rape. Kimberly Peirce's *Boys Don't Cry* treats both coming out as a lesbian and gender bending. Not mainstream, they are filmmakers working in the independent film scene.

Television's Barbara Hall, who created *Joan of Arcadia* and *E.R.*, said it took her awhile to convince program executives that the storyline of *Judging Amy* would have a wide audience, and that a woman writer would be best for the script based on executive producer Amy Brenneman's own experiences with single motherhood. It even incorporates Brenneman's own mother who is a judge in "real" life (Tyne Daly in the series); the judge is a working professional with her own emotional ups and downs—definitely not the stereotypical mom of years past.

Yet these recent bright spots may be just a surface shine.

For there still are problems. The number of women writers, while rising and dropping in alternate years, has not made it past 15 percent in any year through 2004. Some years it may be 13 percent, some years 11 percent. But it has never risen above 15 percent in any year of this new century. Victoria Riskin, past president of the Writers Guild of America West, says, "There's still a prejudice, a bias where women are concerned that you don't hire a woman if you want to do an action picture, which is nonsense. Agents still worry that women are better at writing intimate relationship stories or maybe comedies. [But] There are any numbers of women in the Writers Guild who are highly capable of writing high-action, intense kinds of movies. If anything, they bring perhaps the added value of being able to weave in the relationship components to those high-action films."

The dearth of women screenwriters was of such concern to the Writers Guild of America that in the late 1990s it commissioned a study about women and minorities in the movie business, the Directory of Women Writers. It began, "A common complaint among some film and television producers, directors and other entertainment industry executives is that they don't know many women writers or how to contact them. The Directory solves that problem." Gary Goldstein, the producer of *Pretty Woman*, once said, "Writing may be the one area where there's a tendency towards meritocracy," emphasizing the importance of networking, especially for women. But you can't get a shot at a job if they don't know you're out there.

And at the end of 2002, USC sociology professors Denise and Bill Bielby published their research in which they concluded,

Over the past two decades, women and minorities have made advances in almost every profession. Writing for film and television is a stark exception, where white males continue to dominate the telling of Hollywood's stories. In addition, the relentless pursuit of younger audiences has eroded career opportunities for many older writers, who now find themselves working at the margins of the industry. In short, it's a matter of whose stories get told. Even when we see persons of color or minorities featured in prominent roles in a Hollywood production, the story is almost always told from the perspective of a white, male writer.[3]

Despite these studies, in 2003 only eight of the 100 top grossing films were written by women, and in 2004 the figure dropped to seven.

Things do seem different in a few other countries, such as Australia, New Zealand, Canada, and France. Some have state-supported film programs, and in many cultures a film has high status and is not necessarily the product it so often becomes in America. In France, according to Catherine Breillat, a movie is afforded the same protection and respect as an individual author's work. This has to bring to mind the auteur theory for films created and codified by French critics (sometimes filmmakers) in the *Cahiers du Cinema,* and popularized in America by Andrew Sarris. Perhaps the *auteur* title for director should revert to the screenwriter instead.

Even given some of these discouraging facts and statistics, it is intriguing to see if there is a common theme or thread in women's writing for the screen, particularly those women who get to write what they want and keep it that way. Is their attraction to certain material built in? Is their structure or dialogue definable as "female"? These conjectures used to be dismissed as counter-revolutionary, but this is no longer the case.

A perfect grid on which to place these questions is the work of Barbara Turner, the screenwriter for *Petulia, Pollock,* and *Georgia* (with her daughter Jennifer Jason Leigh in mind). Turner is interviewed in Chapter Four, "Breakaway Queens and Genre Benders."

Other test cases of screenwriters include Jay Presson Allen, a woman who has been in the screenwriting business since the 1950s, when she started in television, and who takes a very dispassionate "it's just a job and a necessarily cooperative one at that" approach to the issue of women writing for movies. Robin Swicord, who has been in the business since the 1980s, takes the opposite tack: not only is the writer's voice crucial and should be consciously attended to, but women screenwriters also should be greatly encouraged, though never kept in a "token" capacity. Naturally, it's hard to discount either of these positions.

Women Screenwriters Today: Their Lives and Words tries to see how women screenwriters' contributions may be affecting not just the shape and content of today's film, but even the movie business itself, a business that considers itself sharing and communal, as women sometimes do. Do women writers get to select material, or are those decisions made by the agents who represent them? And when they do get a topic, are they inclined to give it a female spin? Do they recommend friends, comrades, sisters-in-arms for work?

A side issue, though a more media attention-getting one, has been how women have achieved power and place in the movie business, and how this has affected the products and films they supervise, the people they hire. In the following chapters women writers do not hold back on their sometimes controversial responses to these concerns.

To put some of this in a parable with a historical perspective, if Margaret Mitchell were alive today and there were to be a remake of *Gone With the Wind*, would she be asked to do the script? If a male screenwriter were selected, would it raise some hackles or at least eyebrows?

In fact, the script to the fabled 1939 film was by Sidney Howard, with help from a number of other (male) writers, including F. Scott Fitzgerald, Jo Swerling, and Ben Hecht. Could a woman, or Margaret Mitchell herself, have done better?

To paraphrase Virginia Woolf, if William Goldman had a sister, where would she end up? Doing a deal with Jerry Bruckheimer, or found passed out (or worse) in a tiny office, track-marked arms clutching unpaid bills and rejection letters, sprawled over a brilliant if unproduced script? *Women Screenwriters Today: Their Lives and Words*, by presenting useful advice and giving examples, is designed to promote the former, not the latter, scenario, and to make the mythical Ms. Goldman as settled, successful, and financially stable as her brother William (Goldman, not Shakespeare).

Chapter One

Giving Melodrama a Good Name: The Film of Sensibility

For many years, the film of sensibility—the woman's melodrama of the 1940s, such as a Bette Davis or Joan Crawford film, or the more high-minded *Mrs. Miniver,* or our era's elegant if sometimes precious works of Merchant-Ivory—was ghettoized. It was a glamorous ghetto, of course, whether it housed a high-strung Davis or an elegantly clad Helena Bonham Carter. And while it may have been a big money-maker in the 1940s (Columbia's Harry Cohn geared his product toward the women who picked the films and took their husbands and boyfriends, he always said), it was also a repository/holding tank for women writers such as Lenore Coffee and Catherine Turney.

Thanks, however, to recent movies made from scripts by women writers, the film of sensibility now appeals to moviegoers of taste across the country and across the financial and sexual spectrum. Films including *Little Women, Angela's Ashes, Runaway Bride, The Piano, Sleepless in Seattle,* and *The Big Chill* have had such a wide audience and have experienced such critical success that their appeal has somewhat overshadowed the fact that they belong to the genre of what used to be thought of as "women's movies" or "weepies," and were all written by women screenwriters. In essence, they are about emotional matters, or the interior life of feelings, and are character-driven. Some definitions say women's films simply have females at the center, but others broaden the definition to include issues that only women are faced with, such as being a single mother, or prejudice against women in the workplace.

Films of sensibility, as I am thinking about them here, are—yes—in the genre of women's films. But they also inhabit the emotional ether which surrounds the sensitive and important "new" feelings triggered by our heightened awareness of women's issues and concerns.

Not all films of sensibility have been written (or directed) by women. Both Robert Benton and James Brooks have been known for writing roles for women in their films. But the turning point for feminists, professional cinephiles, and academics such as Joan Mellen and Marjorie Rosen was the 1970s questioning of the image of women in film, generally as presented by male writer-directors. A movie like *Klute*, for instance, was criticized because it showed a prominent female actor only as a hooker. To counteract this, some critics reworked their interpretation of the "women's films" of the 1930s and 1940s, defined by Jeanine Basinger as films where a woman "is at the center of her universe, that her main job in life is just being a woman, and that the woman's film still provides some—probably temporary—liberation from this. Today's women's movies are those where the central problem is particular to being a female."[1]

Other critics today simply see a woman's film as one where a female is the lead, preferably in a part which is either autonomous, or which highlights (and hopefully solves) a problem. And the films of today which are concerned with feelings and with relationships have moved beyond the "weepies" of the past in other ways. Perhaps they have cross-age and cross-gender appeal because men have learned to admit to their feelings.

Or possibly women who have written these films are just that good, and have made movies so appealing that men like them as well.

Still, as one might expect, many of today's films of sensibility or melodrama are movies written by women, sometimes women who came up via the personal or independent film genre. Occasionally they come from women directors nurtured by female-friendly institutional support of film in their native countries.

Angela's Ashes, the adaptation of the Frank McCourt autobiographical tale directed by Jane Campion, was written by Laura Jones, an Australian who first came to international recognition with her script for *An Angel at My Table* which told the story of New Zealand novelist Janet Frame. Some have seen *The Piano* with a script by New

Zealander Campion, who also trained at the AFTRS (Australian Film, Television and Radio School), as the ultimate woman's film of modern times, crossing over to U.S. and international acclaim with Golden Globe and Oscar recognition for original screenplay. Canadian writer-director Cynthia Scott's *The Company of Women* (1991) got attention even in the competitive U.S. market, although its topic was the life and experiences of six female senior citizens.

Sleepless in Seattle, written and directed by Nora Ephron, was such a smash with its comic look at the relationships between the sexes that it nearly developed into a genre by itself: the Ephron urban romantic comedy. As popular as the film was with both sexes, and from coast to coast, it is nevertheless very much a woman's film.

Too sentimental to qualify as pure social comedy, *Sleepless in Seattle* does not shy away from emotional-based issues of women's melodrama (love, motherhood, etc.). Even *The Big Chill* (1983), though strictly speaking not a woman's film, has as its primary theme not the suicide of Alex, as may have been originally intended, or even a portrait of the sixties generation, but the urgent female concern of how to balance the demands of home and family with career achievement. In other words, how to beat the biological clock while still getting your advanced degrees or/and making partner. Trust the work of art, as D. H. Lawrence would say, not the author. The script was by a Hollywood insider, Barbara Benedek (with Lawrence Kasdan); Benedek also wrote *Sabrina* (1995) and *Men Don't Leave* (1990).

These movies have ended up being huge draws for male and female audiences alike. Is this because men have changed, or because the new fashion for a nurturing male has encouraged male interest in issues of sensibility or emotion? Or is it that they have always been concerned about relationship issues, but were too embarrassed or intimidated to admit it? The fast answer to these questions is a simple yes. Some of the underlying reasons for this might be the litigated pressure for the rise of women in the workplace, a media-encouraged awareness of the difficulties of balancing a career and child-rearing, and a generalized New Age questioning of macho values.

More pertinent to our topic: Are women writers needed to successfully treat women's topics? Do some women writers feel obligated for personal or ideological reasons to try? If so, why doesn't "the industry" admit it and hire women this way, right off, without limiting their access to Hollywood or the industry? While no one starts at the top in any industry, of course, why does it seem that women often have to come in very much from the side, sometimes from the independent, sometimes even from a marginally appealing film?

For answers to these questions, fast forward to the women writers themselves, willing and sometimes eager to give their perspective, their point of view. One such forthcoming author is Robin Swicord.

One thing about Swicord: she is not a cardboard cutout feminist thinker. In fact, the author of the scripts for *Little Women*, *The Perez Family*, *Practical Magic*, and other films identified in most people's minds as a writer specializing in women's topics, has a surprisingly sidewise take on women in the film industry.

You'd be hard pressed to say which of Swicord's comments is most unexpected. During an interview in her home in California, she says, "In all honesty, I'm not sure if a woman *can* write a woman's part better than a man. I hate it when something arrives at the door with a note appended, 'You write the girl's role and Nick can write the guy's part.' We call it pink and blue thinking." Nick is Nicholas Kazan, Swicord's husband and occasional writing partner, and the son of controversial director Elia Kazan. Her unique "pink and blue" appraisal leads Swicord to say, after listing all the obviously thought-through difficulties of being a female in the movie business, "Sexism is not as bad for writers in the business as corporate thinking."

For example, these days when there is a "woman's film idea" out and about, says Swicord, the deal will inevitably go to one of five women stars, with Julia Roberts at the top of the list. Then Ron Bass will get first crack at the script, and if that doesn't work out, it will move down the food chain to the other writers on the "official" list.

It is perhaps this ability to take an unprejudiced look at things that allowed Swicord to write the part of Amy in a new and original way: possibly the most challenging of all the characters in *Little Women* to both "get right" and make a bit more attractive than in the novel. In a novel about sisterly sharing and idealism, and a family of principled New England emancipationists, Amy is the only one of the March sisters to express a fondness for material goods and exhibit more than a bit of vanity. As the novel presents her, over a century before the current vogue for independent heroines, Amy always has seemed the least admirable of all the March sisters, stubborn and self-centered if physically attractive and unabashedly searching for a wealthy husband.

Yet Swicord had a different take on Amy, and it is perhaps a prescient one, considering the contented self-acceptance of many young women today. Swicord says that while she was growing up, she identified most with Jo, the common response for readers reacting to this stand-in for the author. Swicord does point out that she has friends who found Meg the character they felt closest to.

Catharine MacKinnon (the feminist theoretician and law professor at the University of Michigan who has written persuasively and provocatively about both sexual harassment and pornography) "gave me an article of hers from the *Yale Law Review*, 'What Is a White Woman?' I began to realize that I had excluded many women from my thinking," says Swicord. "Who am I to say that someone whose values are not mine is a bimbo?"

So Amy, as the Swicord adaptation of the novel presents her, may be self-centered, but—as she tells her sisters in both the novel and film—at least knows her own mind. "It's important in life to know early on what you want in life" is a phrase taken directly from the novel and highlighted in the movie. Swicord says through writing this script she learned a new appreciation for women who see that at a certain point in their lives their youth and physical attractiveness may be the chief thing they have to offer, and simply go with that. (Swicord also gave the more expected point of view, opposing the demonization of career women; i.e., Sigourney Weaver's character in *Working Girl*, who, she points out, "is not really a monster though the film ends up making a caricature of her and her career ambitions.")

Amy in Swicord's script is shown to have her own code of ethics after all, demonstrating as an adult character a wonderful sense of the French word *gravité*. Smoothly, openly, and not manipulatively, she refuses swain Laurie's first offer of marriage because he is too dissolute, and reminds him that she wishes to be loved not for her family, but for herself.

Perhaps more significantly, there is Amy's conversation with her sister Jo during which Amy ferrets out Jo's feelings toward Laurie, a former would-be suitor (though the feelings were not reciprocated).

Amy, in possibly the most radical feminist speech in the novel and not necessarily one which you might expect in a film, when she seeks Jo's permission to marry Laurie, says, "The bonds of sisterhood outlast those of husband and wife."

This is a sentiment in keeping with the points of the novel that Swicord says she tried to emphasize. "Amy Pascal, the studio executive, and I went through the novel and circled passages which supported the three themes we wanted to emphasize: the preservation of family, female ambition, and how—in the face of adversity—to make dreams come true."

The dream of making *Little Women* into another movie (there have been seven earlier versions) was one that both Swicord and Pascal, at that time a Columbia Pictures executive, had entertained for a number of years. Swicord says Pascal packaged the deal around Winona Ryder, who wanted Gillian Armstrong to direct (the Australian who first received major recognition with *My Brilliant Career* in 1979). Producer Denise Di Novi concurred and she brought in Armstrong. This is very reminiscent of the female connections or troupe that dominated the early years of the movie business (Frances Marion writing for Mary Pickford, Catherine Turney writing for Joan Crawford) but as it turns out is quite rare these days, though in a p.c. world it would be fashionable to think otherwise.

Swicord says she had more input into this 1994 film of the Louisa May Alcott story than any other she has written. She, Di Novi, and Pascal were good friends, according to her, and worked well together. The film was shot in Vancouver, but Swicord managed to see dailies on tape in California and make suggestions. And she had input into casting as well, a fairly rare occurrence for a writer these days. Through her friend, producer Julia Chasman (who produced *Quills* and *The Perez Family*), Swicord discovered Claire Danes, she says, for the part of Beth. (Indeed, the script specifically describes Beth as needing to have a "pre-Raphaelite" look, which of course Danes does have.)

In the final production draft for the movie are unusually specific instructions from Swicord for a scene, ultimately cut due to "budget compression." For instance, when Jo goes to New York to find and make her fortune, the scene first takes us to a part of town where the script instructs descriptively: "Ragged CHILDREN sell kindling from a barrel, not far from another kind of commerce: a bruised CHILD PROSTITUTE [Casting note: played by one of the Hummel children, for subliminal effect] is pimped by her UNSAVORY FA-THER."

The Hummels are the family the Marches rescue with their Christmas dinner in Swicord's script (the Hummel baby being the one Beth nurses when it has scarlet fever, a disease Beth ultimately dies from), and the implication is that without the Marches—committed and idealistic transcendentalists—this would be the fate of the Hummel children, too. According to Swicord, "When the film was shot and edited and we all looked at it, Gillian's placement of the first scene was better than what I first had in my first draft." Swicord opened the movie originally with a scene of the March sisters acting at home in one of Jo's plays, an actual scene in the novel, but it was changed to the return of Marmee after her day of work handing out charity baskets. Swicord says she picked up ways that girls play and interact from watching her own two girls.

The collaboration with Armstrong, Di Novi, and Pascal that Swicord describes with high enthusiasm has not always been her usual experience. Citing not-great experiences with other features, particularly with *Practical Magic* and *The Perez Family*, Swicord's main complaint seems to be that she has had little control or input into most of the movies made from the scripts she has written. "I feel that not to have more writer's input very much hurt both *Practical Magic* and *The Perez Family*."

A graduate of Florida State University, Swicord, who is a Florida native, worked in journalism before coming to New York City with the desire to become a screenwriter. To support herself, she wrote advertising copy, and had a play produced off-Broadway. The theater critic Marilyn Stasio (who now writes for *Variety*) gave her play a good review, and Swicord was encouraged by an agent, Merilly Kane (who still represents her), to move to Los Angeles. The feeling was that Swicord was enough of a new voice, and Kane got her a contract to write a screenplay, *Stock Cars for Christ*. "I was put up in the Del Capri Hotel with a pink typewriter," laughs Swicord. Not too long after moving to the West Coast, Swicord met fellow screenwriter (and sometime director) Nicholas Kazan, who lived in her neighborhood.

Both writers worked at home, as they do now, and serendipitously met due to a similar workout routine.

Like most writers, Swicord says she writes best in the morning: "I guess it sounds like an embarrassment of riches, but in some ways the worst part is that we may both not have a lull at the same time: when I'm busy, Nick isn't and often the other way around, too. Sometimes there is no one to play with."

She spent six months researching *Little Women*, even reading German romantic works and transcendentalist writings which she says paralleled the women's progressive emancipation movement (interests of the March family). She says *The Perez Family*, her next film, required less research, though she went to Miami for background on the Christine Bell novel. "I wrote a very wild first draft including scenes featuring Santaria, the Spanish cult religion. But Mira Nair came on board as a director. After it became her project, she was bent on making a very different film. My access became extremely truncated," laments Swicord.

Trini Alvarado, whom Swicord championed for the role of Meg for *Little Women*, was familiar to Nair, who had worked with Alvarado when she was a young girl; Alvarado was included in the cast of *The Perez Family*.

And there are a number of wonderful, very writerly touches in the script, lines which—notwithstanding Swicord's comments about not wishing to be identified as a "woman writer"—still show what might be called a feminine sensibility. On page four of the script, describing the Miami setting, the POV instructs:

The new moon hangs there, its dark fullness outlined with a glimmering corona. Venus drops jewel-like from the moon's crescent. And in Cuba—

INT: TINY CUBAN PRISON CELL. NIGHT.

Juan Raul stares out of his window slot, at the same moon and starry sky; one hand firmly gripping his wrist, as he silently counts his pulse.

Clearly, a man could write this, but there is a filigree of delicate description that perfectly fits the format of film: simultaneity perhaps being a natural mindset for females, if one is to accept the dicta and observations of Carol Gilligan in A *Different Voice*, that women see the world differently from men, using a language of interconnectedness and interpersonal continuity. Leaving aside for a moment the irony of the word continuity as an early cinematic term, to think of others, to envision scenes occurring at the same moment, by cross-cutting, may be natural for women.

Swicord says that her experience with the 1998 film *Practical Magic* was the most disappointing of all her feature film experiences to date. What should have been an ideal project for a female writer—the adaptation of a novel by Alice Hoffman about witchcraft—turned sour, she says. Actor-director Griffin Dunne directed the film, and in Swicord's words, the film "was taken away from me." Another problem, she believes, is that the director came to the project too late so that, in her words "we could not get 'on the same page' in the time allotted." Additionally, all the decision making power was in his court.

Swicord, who like her husband is extremely active in the Writers Guild, has concluded that the reason many films today are not very good is that the writer, whether male or female, has little or no power. After the Hollywood blacklist, she explains, writers solidified their base in television rather than in movies, and weakened studios were picked off by corporations who still control what they are not ashamed to present as "product."

Still, there are clever dialogue and bits in the script for *Practical Magic* even if—as is generally agreed—the movie turned out to be a bit of a mess. For instance, there is the quasi-feminist but still humorous speech given by Sally Owens (Sandra Bullock) at the end of the movie. Here is a description from the actual script itself, followed by dialogue.

Sally picks up the books and sees with a sickening jolt: "THE BOOK OF BLACK MAGICK," and "HISTORY OF WITCHCRAFT," its cover a WOODCUT of Satan surrounded by debauched Puritan women.

SALLY OWENS
Well. I see you've been reading up on us.
(reads from the book sardonically)
"A talisman held forth in the hand will ward off the Devil."

GARY HALLET
Is that what you're involved in?
Some kind of devil worship?

SALLY OWENS
There's no Devil in the Craft. That was just some bizarre
fantasy on the part of the medieval Bishops. They couldn't
imagine a society of women that wasn't centered around a
man of some kind. Sort of funny—unless you happen to be
tied to the stake.

Or early in the script when the Aunts (Stockard Channing and
Dianne Wiest) gossip about one of their own who has married her
fourth husband:

AUNT FRANCES
Useless. Not a practical bone in her body.

AUNT JET
Not that that's wrong. Darling girl.

AUNT FRANCES
But it doesn't add up to children.
No one to carry on The Craft.

The Aunts gaze pointedly at Sally, their last remaining hope for matriarchal longevity. Sally notices her coffee spoon still stirring round
and round, magically. She puts out a finger to stop it.

SALLY OWENS
I want a normal life, with a nice
Normal man, in a nice normal house.

AUNT JET
Uh! A milquetoast thing to want.

And then Aunt Frances finishes the scene with a Mae West–like
zinger: "My dear, goodness is not a virtue. It's a lack of courage." In

this script, matriarchal myths are referred to by phrases like "Great Hecuba!"

Swicord's other scripts include *Matilda*, a children's film directed by Danny DeVito which she cowrote with Kazan, and *Shag*. Swicord says, as might be expected, that she enjoyed writing with her husband and would like to do that again. But she has decided that producing-directing her own films is the way to go in order to keep control over a project, maintain the vision she has for her films, and be happy with the final product.

This is not a unique concept or statement, and has also been expressed by any number of women screenwriters including Callie Khouri, screenwriter for the breakthrough smash *Thelma and Louise*, writer-director for *The Divine Secrets of the Ya-Ya Sisterhood*, and Nora Ephron. In fact while Ephron does still write or cowrite a script, directing seems her chief interest, a position Khouri also takes. Swicord recently wrote and directed her own independent production, *The Mermaids Singing*, shot in Ireland. And she shares credit with Akiva Goldsman, Ron Bass, and Doug Wright for the script to *Memoirs of a Geisha*, adapted from the Arthur Golden novel. Was Swicord hired for this film because of her "woman's touch"?

Swicord's story may be a bit atypical in its "Cinderalla-ish quality," at least in her outline. That is, there were some years of struggle for her—living for a time in a crummy apartment in New York and even taking welfare while perfecting her craft. But once she had a play produced and she connected with her longtime agent, she has at least worked consistently, though like numerous writers worries about the corporate culture which started to infiltrate studios around the time she came on the scene, she says. Swicord is not the only screenwriter primarily thought of as a writer of women's parts.

Laura Jones, the screenwriter from Sydney, Australia, built an entire reputation writing films about women (generally adaptations), making an international career breakthrough with a 1990 TV miniseries directed by Jane Campion, *An Angel at My Table*. Jones worked with director Gillian Armstrong in 1987 in her original script for *High Tide* about a reunion between a woman (Judy Davis) and her adopted-away daughter. Since then, all of Jones' work has been adaptations of novels with strong female characters: *The Portrait of a Lady*, directed by Campion, *The Well*, an Australian thriller featuring two headstrong women, *Oscar and Lucinda*, the adaptation of Peter Carey's Booker Prize–winning novel, and *A Thousand Acres*, centering on three sisters quarreling about their inheritance. She was also pegged to adapt Frank McCourt's *Angela's Ashes*.

Numerous critics have called *An Angel at My Table* a perfect example of a film that's strongly within the genre of a woman's film. Adapted from Jane Frame's novel, it was first a television miniseries. After a great success, it was fashioned into a feature film. It highlights a woman's drive to become a writer in a patriarchal, sometimes hostile environment, and nothing is glossed over, including Frame's breakdown and treatment for schizophrenia. Her breakdown actually features one of the movie's cleverest and most matter-of-factly delivered lines; when Janet arrives home to her family in the bush to report her diagnosis, she announces, "I've got schizophrenia" (as if you could catch it, like the measles). Hardly standard pop fare. The film does not whitewash the rather barbaric medical practices of that time, her brief early affair and a doomed pregnancy, and of course wonderfully highlights her struggles to find her voice as a writer.

Visually speaking, the movie is experimental, too, skewing its images toward "woman's reality." Though it sounds like a trite detail (it's not), there's a detail on which—one dares to say—only a female writer-director team might focus: Frame's out-of-control and attention-getting bright red frizzy hair—the perfect emblem for her particular female concerns.

She and others try to deal with her hair that is shown to be a real attention-getting problem for this painfully shy young woman, and there are funny scenes as her classmates try to arrange and control "Fuzzy's" hair, as she was nicknamed. Hair is an issue for women, of course, but the filmmakers also use it to highlight Frame's irrepressible nature belied by her quiet exterior. Her hair will not conform to the basic styles acceptable at the time, and keeps popping through at all the wrong moment it seems. Even today, if you visit New Zealand, you will see proudly displayed in numerous bookstores and coffeehouses the series of photos of the three perfectly matched red-haired actresses who played Frame at various intervals in her life.

All of this brings up the complicated issue of the contribution of the screenwriter to the final form of a film; in interviews Jones has said how closely she likes to work with directors, and how strongly she believes in the importance of having the writer on the set.

A less successful investigation of particular female issues, including marriage versus personal freedom, is seen in *Portrait of a Lady*, which received mixed if "respectable" reviews. The script (and film) take pains to present Isabel Archer's state of emotional confusion with numerous dark sequences indicating her perceptual dilemmas: who to trust, why, and why not. While some of this may not have made for easy or uncomplicated viewing, these dark sequences did definitely indicate a mood of moral ambiguity, one that both writer and director determined to emphasize.

Though they are not exclusive partnerships, the Armstrong-Jones and the Campion-Jones relationships demonstrate the same kind of creative cross-fertilization seen in the early era of the movie business in the United States, and as nostalgically praised in some of Swicord's projects. It has the feel—at least at this writing—of being a company, if loosely organized and with replaceable parts.

One reason for this may be that the Australian Film Commission is very active in encouraging women's (and alternative) women's cinema. Another might be that Jones, quoted in a recent Australian Writers Guild report, has said, "Moral rights are important to me in that they reflect my work on a film. They acknowledge the integral part of a screenplay in the film-making process. Both writer and director are the author of a film."

Unhappily for American films and audiences, these types of creative partnerships are simply not so long-lasting in Hollywood. Unlike the early days when a June Mathis was in place long enough to hire a Frances Marion to write a script, power bases are too slippery and hard to hang onto. Denise Di Novi, for instance, is no longer in power at Paramount and so is not in a position to push through or at least approve many of the women's projects she signed on during her tenure. A few female directors, such as Betty Thomas, may not get assigned a female writer necessarily, or even the same writer over again, as when Dorothy Arzner or Lois Weber might connect over and over with the same writer.

So it seems that the interesting kind of collaboration that Swicord has described in the making of *Little Women* may be a rarity. While it is encouraging to read, as the *New York Times* tells us on May 1, 2005, that there are more women in executive positions of power in the movie business than anywhere else, and it should be regarded therefore as a statistical model, the spillover does not necessarily trickle down to hiring women writers on extending their influence.

Instead, things seem to be more in line with a description by Jay Presson Allen, scriptwriter for *Just Tell Me What You Want, The Prime of Miss Jean Brodie, Prince of the City*, and *Marnie*. "If you don't work very closely with a director, you're not going to see anything you want up on the screen. There's no way. So you had better invite the gentleman to piss a little on the script. Put his mark on it. Make it his." (This frequently-published quote was stylistically modified when I interviewed Allen; she says she simply meant that a director to be worth his or her salt has to put so much time into a project that they must feel it is fully theirs.)

Still the questions remain: Is the impulse to dominate creatively (or just dominate) a particularly male one? How does directing fit into this picture?

Is the impulse to control (the director's impulse) similar to assertiveness? Virginia Woolf took this up more eloquently nearly a century ago in *A Room of One's Own*, commenting on the "phallocentric pen" and the male ego unafraid to mark or dominate a page, a blank sheet of paper, a new continent, and so forth. And here, of course, a blank screen. One angle is given by Lisa Loomer, who was one of the writer/adaptors for one of the chief female melodramas of our time— *Girl, Interrupted*. (The others were Anna Hamilton Phelan and James Mangold.) "In the film business," she says, "I am more a 'writer for hire.' And too often a movie I've written or rewritten does not get made. I'm not used to that as a playwright, and no matter how many times it happens to me as a screenwriter it does not make sense to me. People tell me, 'Well you got paid, didn't you?' But I still can't believe that something I've put my heart into—and gotten paid well for—just sits on a shelf." And with just a tinge of anger, Loomer says,

I was the original writer on the movie. I wrote two drafts. After that, it was out of my hands. When you see different people credited on a film, and the word "and" between their names, it means they all wrote separate drafts. If you see an ampersand between two names it means they worked together. I had no role in the casting. I never met the director. I got the job in the usual way. I was asked to come in and "pitch" a story based on the book—which is basically a series of vignettes, musings, and essays. There is no plot. I made up a "story," chose the protagonist, and created the antagonist—all based on what I perceived to be the theme of the book. I got the job based on this "pitch." What you saw on film, by the way, is quite different from what I wrote.

Loomer also reports, "I spent a great deal of time with [author] Susanna Kayser before I started writing. As far as I know, she was never involved in the writing of the movie." *Girl, Interrupted* is the autobiographical story by Kayser of her time in a mental institution in the 1960s.

Loomer, who has written extensively for the theater and television, grew up in New York. But she says that it is necessary to be in Los Angeles to get into the business. "You have to be here to write series television. Of course, it can be dangerous for a writer to live in L.A. because that can become your frame of reference. The only difficulty I experience is that I get offered a lot of 'women's' projects—coming-of-age stories, romances. Don't get me wrong. I have nothing against 'women's stories'—I'd like to see more of them. I just don't like to be typecast as a writer."

When I spoke to Loomer, she was writing a pilot for the television channel Showtime based on her 2003 play *Living Out*. Like so many writers of both sexes, Loomer says she works best in the morning, and fastest on deadline, but does not assign herself a set number of pages to complete in a day. "I try to work fairly consistently because I believe that writing is a craft that can be honed. I also believe that the best writing comes *through us* in some sense, and that the 'muse' or whatever you want to call it, is something to be open to—but not forced. Some of my best ideas come in the middle of the night or on a walk, when I am not 'writing' at all."

Girl, Interrupted is firmly within the tradition of a woman's film, or melodrama, with its focus on emotion. Possibly one of the reasons for the film's success would be what you might call the emotion-driven nature of Loomer's drive to create, at least as she describes it. "Write the story that only you know. Understand 'form,' structure. Then write that thing you're afraid will be too weird for anyone else to possibly get, not what you think will get made. Right now, I'm more interested in why someone stays in the business without getting broken—than in how they 'break in.' "

Sounds an awful lot like the women in *Girl, Interrupted*.

Reading the film criticism of the feminist writers of the 1970s, one senses a kind of apologetic tone for giving a feminist spin to melodrama, a form looked down upon since Richardson's *Clarissa* and *Pamela*, and subsequently scorned through the nineteenth century gothic novels like *Wuthering Heights* or *Jane Eyre*. Yet women screenwriters today seem to have no such problem. Melodrama is nothing to be ashamed of. In fact, as its basis is emotion, it is a form to be exercised for every good female end.

Another case in point is Canadian filmmaker Patricia Rozema, who broke ground with her highly original and lesbian-themed *I've Heard the Mermaids Singing* in 1987, and which won the Prix de la Jeunesse at the Cannes Film Festival. She also wrote and directed *The White Room* and *When Night Is Falling*, a critically acclaimed modern retelling of the myth of Cupid and Psyche. Her short feature *Bach Cello Suite No. 6: Six Gestures* was one of a sextet of short films with the cellist Yo-Yo Ma, for which she was awarded an Emmy and the Golden Rose of Montreux in 1997.

At first Rozema seems an odd choice for Miramax producer Harvey Weinstein to have made for *Mansfield Park*.[2] The less-than-glitzy Rozema lives in Toronto, can take as much as seven years between projects (she explains during a junket for the movie that her "lifestyle is not high end"), and is mainly known for her work in the independent film industry. She says she sent her original script for the film to Weinstein, who bought it.

She may have been the perfect writer for *Mansfield Park*, the last of the Jane Austen novels to be made into a movie at the end of the twentieth century. Some say this is the least accessible of all of Austen's novels—and therefore obviously the least likely to offend if deviated form. More to the point, perhaps, *Mansfield Park* is a novel Austen herself considered radical, experimental. For just one thing, it takes a critical view of the slave-based business of Sir Thomas, which supports his family and Mansfied Park. But though it is in the background of the Austen text, Rozema has brought it to the fore, including scenes which focus on graphic, quasi-pornographic sketches of miscegenational couplings, usually between master and slave.

"From the beginning," Rozema told me, "I didn't want to do another Jane Austen garden party. I wanted to show the passion of Jane Austen, her fierce humanity, her devastating wit, and her deep-seated belief in the power of love between two people." Typically Austen, the heroine must make a choice between a man of money or a man of values—not always the same thing in her novels, although it happily was for the heroine of *Pride and Prejudice*. Rozema spent many months reading Jane Austen's letters, mining them for dialogue, anecdotes, and finding source material for structural changes for her script. "The thing that really attracted me about Austen's own letters was their lively tone. She originally wrote them to amuse her family and friends and Austen's humor shines through." Consequently, Rozema acknowledges, the "new" Fanny is a hybrid: part the principled character of Austen's creation and part Austen herself. As Fanny comes of age, she becomes a headstrong writer, a "wild beast" as Austen once described herself. And indeed there are many scenes showing Fanny scribbling in her notebook.

One of the most obvious (and most commented on) original insertions coming from Rozema was the lesbian interpretation given to the relationship between Mary Crawford (Embeth Davidtz in the film) and Fanny Price (Frances O'Connor). Rozema's answer is that "Mary Crawford is a woman who wants a taste of everything, who has enormous appetites. She's not so much depraved as she is forward-thinking, always looking to the next move. Embeth had the strength and the charm to capture that. She's a very sophisticated actress who works with a finely-tuned clarity."

Yet she, and her films, are taken seriously. Of all the social comedies of Austen, *Mansfield Park* is the closest to melodrama, with its heroine plagued by adversity in its gothic glow. The lesbian advances only add a layer of intrigue, and in some ways Rozema has made a very high level "woman in jeopardy" film.

And yet when asked if women write differently for movies, or if gender makes a difference in writing for the screen, Rozema, in an interview in the fall of 1999, answered with a simple, straightforward, "No." (Her colleague and fellow Canadian Suzette [Suzie] Le Coutre, interviewed in the upcoming chapter about television writers, laughed when I told her this; she reminded me that perhaps Rozema was thinking she didn't want to cut herself out of any work.)

Rozema's work is supported and promoted by the Film Board of Canada. She says that she has not experienced any particular prejudice in the film business, or in getting into the industry. As she lives outside Toronto, and her needs are relatively simple, Rozema says she need not produce any set number of films in order to survive, and therefore probably has had fewer clashes with film people in power.

For just as women's novels were once disparaged and dismissed in the nineteenth century as unimportant because they only dealt with minor matters of the heart, or emotion, this was once also the case for movies with similar themes. And the parallels continues. No one today would dare dismiss a fiction work like *Jane Eyre*; just so, a movie like *Girl, Interrupted* is taken most seriously.

The whole idea of chick flicks is no longer laughable. And its rarefied subtype—the film of emotion, sensibility, melodrama, or whatever name or category critics create—is no longer to be dismissed as lightweight.

Chapter Two

Vets and Lifers:
How They Got and Stayed In

A number of critically and commercially successful films have come from women screenwriters in recent years. It is perhaps no accident that many of these successes have come from lifers, or "vets" in the business—women who broke through, somehow, and stuck it out, such as Elaine May (*Primary Colors* and *The Birdcage*), Nora Ephron (*Sleepless in Seattle*), Anna Hamilton Phelan (*Gorillas in the Mist*), Naomi Foner (*Losing Isaiah* and *Running on Empty*), Barbara Benedek (*The Big Chill* and *Men Don't Leave*), Melissa Mathison (*E.T.*), Gloria Katz (*Indiana Jones and the Temple of Doom*), and Jay Presson Allen (*Marnie* and *The Prime of Miss Jean Brodie*).

None of these women are novices, nor, in movie industry terms anyway, are they young. And while they may have gained entry through unusual circumstances—the sisters Ephron, for instance, Nora and Delia, are the daughters of the well-known screenwriting team Phoebe and Henry Ephron; Elaine May had entrée because of her famous Second City skits with Mike Nichols in Chicago—they have still managed longevity in a very insecure work environment.

In the demise of the studio system, with "Hollywood's" corporate culture, and a few (though very few) significant stars commanding money and power, these writers may be—though they remain free-lancers, working out of their homes or their own offices—the clos-est thing the movie business has today to a stable of writers who have been around for a while. Not exactly old warhorses, they still are turned to in times of trouble: both May and Allen are well-known, for instance, for script doctoring, or fixing a movie that is in trouble.

Still, they are most definitely not working within the safety net of the old studio system, which, whatever its deficits, insecurities, and interferences, at least presented some idea of a workplace, even if that workplace might be cleared out overnight, as many industry veterans have described in tales whether literal or embellished. That they have survived and have kept writing for decades in this most tenuous of work situations is a testament to their talent and stamina.

Elaine May is one writer who sidled into the screenwriting trade with an already established reputation made over thirty years ago, a vet before she even got into movies. Famous for her work as a sketch writer for Second City, along with her writing partner Mike Nichols whom she met at the University of Chicago, where they put together an improvisational group called the Compass, the team moved to New York, where they had great success on Broadway. May then decided to try her hand alone in Hollywood. For a while it seemed that Nichols' prediction that she would be miserable in the movie business (as her work would be out of her control) proved false.

Her first work was as an actress in the film *Enter Laughing*, and then *Luv*. She went to writing and directing, in the comic satire *A New Leaf* (1971), which she adapted from a short story she had optioned. So May started at a point many Hollywood writers only strive for. *A New Leaf* is a gentle-edged comedy, the story of a bumbling, wealthy scientist (May), courted by a gigolo played by Walter Matthau, who weds her and, eventually in spite of himself, falls in love with her. In fact, it is the kind of "little" relationship film—though a far superior one—that some contemporary independent filmmakers claim to have developed as an antidote to huge blockbuster and action movies.

Because her next directorial effort, *Mikey and Nicky*, was an organizational and financial disaster, May wasn't given another chance to work in Hollywood for ten years. But she redeemed herself by writing the script for the remake of *Heaven Can Wait*, starring Warren Beatty. Once more into the breach with the disastrous *Ishtar*, which May also directed, and since then her movie writing successes have all been exclusively due to her writing.

Primary Colors was a smash; the same was true for *The Birdcage*. Of course the director for both those films was Mike Nichols, a return to that extraordinarily successful partnership. Though she received no credit, May was also a screenwriter for Beatty's *Reds* (1981) and Sydney Pollack's *Tootsie* (1982). And while these films may be "progressive" in theme and content, as she has written and structured them, she says there was no conscious effort to write particularly strong parts for women, or to deliberately write for women. (May did however direct, though not write, *The Heartbreak Kid* for her daughter Jeannie Berlin.)

This is not, however, the case with another industry "vet," screenwriter Anna Hamilton Phelan. A frequent participant in "women and film" panels and a widely quoted writer, Phelan is the creator of two highly etched, extraordinary parts for women: that of a single mother in *Mask* (1985), played with freewheeling, ass-kicking energy by Cher, and that of Dian Fossey in *Gorillas in the Mist* in 1988, a role played with sensitivity and physical daring by Sigourney Weaver. Phelan also is one of three credited writers on *Girl, Interrupted*, the 1999 hit starring Winona Ryder and Angelina Jolie.

A former actress, Phelan says in a tongue-in-cheek way that she decided to become a screenwriter when she was in a television film as a dance hall girl and the producer recast her as the madam. After that, she has selected or been selected for movies that focus on women's parts, experiences, and preferences. She says "The question of responsibility is a balance that I struggle with all the time in my work. I have an enormous sense of responsibility to my gender. And about race. As I get older, I realize it's part of my being. It's not going to go away. So I just go with it and do the best I can. Sigourney Weaver once said to me, 'Anna, if you and other writers stop writing about female characters, then our daughters and granddaughters will have no female images on the screen to identify with at all.' That's an enormous obligation."

Phelan is also among those who foresaw the importance of residuals for writers and that they were getting screwed in that regard: "Some writers from the Writers Guild of America were not getting foreign revenues owed them for episodes they had written of *I Love Lucy*, which were now being shown in India. The producer told them that there were no revenues coming from that country, that no one in India watched that show. Shortly after that, someone from the Writers Guild happened to be in a little village in India and noticed that many

21

of the children were named Lucy, Ricky, Ethel, and Fred. That was the beginning of a lawsuit, so these writers could get what was due them."[1]

Regarding the women characters she has created, Phelan says, "I'm especially attracted to women who are mouthy and unsympathetic on the outside, but who hide cores of insecurity. It's become obvious to me over the years that this kind of woman reflects both the changes she wishes to have, and help make, in the world, as well as the forces that have impacted on her in the past."

Like most screenwriters, Phelan says she works best in the very early morning, and likes to write to music. For *Mask*, her inspiration was the songs "War Pigs" and "Iron Man" from Black Sabbath, Springsteen tunes during the writing of *Gorillas in the Mist*, and Jayhawks songs during work on *Girl, Interrupted*, a film on which she shares credit.

But perhaps the most interesting thing Phelan has to say about *Mask* is that it was triggered by her training as an actress: For instance, in the case of Rocky Dennis, the main character of *Mask*, he was in the waiting room of a hospital where she was doing theater work. "This comes from what I'm sure is my background in acting. I put on a doctor's lab coat, and went in and introduced myself. I said, 'You must really have a story to tell.' Now that I think about it, it was really brazen, but it really helped."

Another highly versatile writer who has been on the scene for quite a while is Melissa Mathison, the writer of one of the greatest audience-reachers and moneymakers of all time, *E.T.* (which was also edited by a highly experienced editor, Carol Littleton). Mathison was also the scriptwriter for the children's film *Indian in the Cupboard, The Escape Artist*, and *Kundun*, the epic about a child emperor.

My guess is that Mathison, as a woman writer, significantly added to the emotional pathos of what otherwise could be seen as a sci-fi film, for it's the homeward yearnings of the childlike E.T. that gets to the audience. It is simply impossible to determine exactly how much this layer added, and of that how much had to do with a female sensibility. But there does seem to be something there: "E.T. phone home" is even more poignant than Dorothy in *The Wizard of Oz* saying, "There's no place like home."

Here is a thumbnail sketch of Mathison's background and rise in the movie business, an entry only too familiar sounding to those who peg nepotism and personal contacts as the usual way to make it in the movie business, a seeming reality for even those who eventually out-pace their connections. The daughter of a Southern Californian jour-nalist father and part-time publicist mother, Mathison went to the University of California at Berkeley and worked as a stringer from San Francisco for *Time* magazine, a job she got through one of her father's contacts. She took a leave of absence from Berkeley to work with Francis Ford Coppola (for whose family she had been a babysitter) to work as an assistant on *The Godfather Part II*. Coppola prodded her to write and a few years later set her to work on *The Black Stallion*. Mathison says, "We agreed the movie should be like a children's book, with just pictures. That's when I learned to take out the words, to tell the story visually, which is the best training there is."

It's an open secret that Mathison and Francis Coppola were an item, even referred to in Eleanor Coppola's book *Notes*, about the making of *Apocalypse Now*. Eventually Mathison hooked up with Harrison Ford and was with him in Tunisia for the making of *Raiders of the Lost Ark* when the director, Steven Spielberg, asked her to sub-mit an idea for a film about a visitor from outer space. Mathison says that both she and Spielberg wanted E.T. to be found by children, and that writing dialogue for them was easy enough: "I'm very good at lis-tening to kids. I talk like them anyway." While it was no problem to think of her audience as a 14-year-old boy, she also asked children what they would like E.T. to be like (the most common answer was for him to be telepathic).

Interestingly, Mathison insists that she did not write science fiction. "It may be fantasy but it's not science fiction. We were rather against that. The space ship is so silly. We wanted it to look like a Christmas tree ornament. It's not high tech and it's not sophisticated. It's rusty and pretty and simple and the creatures inside it are benevolent little gardeners."

She says her writing method is to simply write through while there is momentum, and then go back and rewrite. *E.T.* was a co-authorship with Spielberg, with whom she works well because sometimes "our sentences are almost identical. His idea was this nice little person gets stranded on Earth. And from then on we collaborated about that. I would go home and write for a week and then come down and see him where he was editing *Raiders*, tell him what I'd worked on, we'd throw it around for a couple of hours and then I'd go home and work for another week."

Mathison says she personally has not encountered discrimination in the movie business because of being a woman, though she allows, "It's true in general, but not for me. Being a woman never had any relevance, one way or another. I'm not political, but it is true, women are second-rate in the movie industry."

From the point of view of female (and writers') gains in the movie business, a little known but highly significant fact is the watershed win achieved by Mathison and the Writers Guild. Through arbitration, Mathison won a share of *E.T.*'s massive merchandising revenues. The arbitrator determined that she would receive four to five percent of all the company's revenue from toys, dolls, clothing, and other items that feature the character of E.T., deeming it a "unique and original" creation. The ruling declared: "If Mathison's E.T. had been less detailed, then Universal's position would have merit. However, Mathison had extensively detailed her main character in her first two working drafts, before the model by Carlo Rimaldi. Mathison did not stop at writing only that E.T.'s finger glowed. She described the character's unique hands and fingers. Mathison did not only write that E.T. was three-and-a-half feet tall; she created short squashed legs, a telescopic neck, a protruding belly, long, thin arms and a glowing heart. She did not simply write that E.T.'s face was round, but detailed his wide head, the softness in his face, his large, round eyes, the leathery creases and furrows in his brow."

Though the decision was dependent upon a merchandising provision in the WGA contract, the award also spells out the importance of detailed description from a writer, finding her or his signature, a position at odds with the usual dicta of writing lean for scripts. A win like this, as well as giving financial security, also makes the victor a solid presence in the small but powerful film community. Here is someone to be reckoned with, one way or another, and with a credibility that can only contribute to longevity in the business.

One woman writer on the scene in Los Angeles since the late 1980s who is proudly straightforward about her deliberate use of a female point of view and creation of strong women characters is Naomi Foner, a screenwriter who had a breakthrough film, *Running on Empty*, in 1988. It gave her, in her own words, "a little corner on character-based movies." The movie starred Christine Lahti and Judd Hirsch as a radical 1960s couple who have gone underground; they are hiding out because of their anti-government activities earlier. One of their sons (played by the late River Phoenix, in an Oscar-nominated turn) in particular wants to end their covert, nomadic existence. Though most critics pegged *Running* as primarily showing generational conflict, Foner maintains it is really a film about family, joking that "parenthood is the only love affair in which separation is a happy ending."

Foner believes being identified as a character-based writer is synonymous with being thought of as a woman's writer. She wrote *Violets Are Blue* in 1986 starring Sissy Spacek, *A Dangerous Woman* (Debra Winger) in 1993, and *Losing Isaiah* (Jessica Lange and Halle Berry) in 1995. As of this writing, Foner is the writer for a movie in development, *Grace*, to star Sandra Bullock, about Grace Metalious, the author of *Peyton Place*.

Foner's career in the movie business, however, started in the 1970s with her work on *Sesame Street* and a program called *Visions* on public television in New York City. A graduate of Barnard College, Foner says the work she did as a television producer was a perfect platform for her subsequent career progress, and what she calls "political in the broadest sense. I evolved the trickle-up theory. That is if people *felt* something, they might actually *do* something about it. I could have written polemic, but I truly felt—still do—that the best way to effect social change is through people's emotions. I'm sure Anne Frank reached more people with her story than any number of statistics. Plus, my experience in public television was the best training I could possibly have for being a screenwriter."

She also adds that because of this progressive platform she encountered no resistance due to her sex. Rather, her hesitancy to start writing scripts was more personal: "I spent a lot of time working with writers during those years," she says, "but was afraid to pen anything myself because I didn't want to find out that I couldn't do it. Finally, a friend insisted and since it coincided with the birth of my daughter, I tried. It was produced on PBS' *Visions* series."

This event coincided with her personal philosophy: she did not start to write scripts full time until she had her first child (Maggie Gyllenhaal), because she wanted to stay at home and did not like the idea of someone else raising her child. "I'm fortunate that I came from a family where there have always been professional women: aunts who were doctors and so forth. There was never any question that I would do a career something, but I eschewed the idea of shelving motherhood, as was the feminist fashion for my generation." (In fact, one of her children, Jake Gyllenhaal, is achieving mainstream status as an actor, starring in *Bubble Boy* in 2001 and having taken parts in *October Sky* in 1999. Other credits of his are *Donnie Darko*, *The Good Girl*, and *The Day After Tomorrow*. He played roles in Foner's scripts for *A Dangerous Woman* and *Running on Empty*. The screenwriter's daughter, Maggie Gyllenhaal, has also achieved numerous screen successes, including *Riding in Cars with Boys* in 2001, *Secretary* in 2002, and *The Great New Wonderful* in 2005. She also was in *Donnie Darko* with brother Jake.)

Foner's break into the feature film business came when she and her director husband, Stephen Gyllenhaal, moved from New York, driving across the country to Los Angeles. "[Stephen] had finished a film and wanted to show it around." She does point out, however, that once in L.A., people assumed that her career success came because her husband was in the business. This never happened in New York, she says.

At some point, Foner recalls, she realized that "I've really been writing the same story over and over. It's been an unconscious crusade. Women's stories need to be told." She points out, however, that in her experience it is much more difficult these days to make a movie about a woman. "The studio producers are only interested in targeting an audience of men between 18 and 25. You simply can't make a film with one female in the central role."

Foner says she does not believe that women and men write differently. "Good writers, men and women alike, simply pay more attention to details." Like many writers interviewed for this book, Foner believes that the best time to write is in the morning, the closest you can get to the unconscious or dream state. "Many times a problem I've been working on seems to be solved when I wake up in the morning."

One difference that she does see between men and women in the business is that "I think men will do anything to get their films made. Women seem to understand *process* better. They tend to be more concerned with people's feelings. Some of my favorite producers are women who can get the job done but without being totally tyranni-cal."

I interviewed Foner by telephone from her office in Los Angeles. Foner says it's best for her to work away from home, though in fact an office may just be at times a makeshift table in a little room near her house. "Lately some of the best writing I've done has been in the Beverly Hills Library. There was all this productive work going on around me. Otherwise it can be a bit, well, lonely."

One of Foner's favorite actresses to work with is Debra Winger, who has the reputation of being difficult. According to Foner, Winger is harder on herself than anyone else, and will turn herself inside out for the work. Winger took the part of the mentally challenged lead in *A Difficult Woman*. "She wants the best. It's not about vanity on every level. She wants everybody up to their highest standards. That kind of difficult is fine with me."

Because she was executive producer on most of her films, Foner has had some control over the final product, a rarity in movies these days she says. She strongly believes that the writer should be on the set, and an active participant in the filmmaking process. "It's important to be on hand, to work with the actor. Sometimes you can write dia-logue and when you see the actor doing the lines, they already own the character and you realize that some of the language may be re-dundant."

A positive example of being on the set as the writer, she says, was working with Sidney Lumet, a director lauded by many writers and the recipient of an Oscar for Lifetime Achievement in 2005. "He would turn to me and ask if a change could be made," Foner observes, adding how special that is from a director.

She recently adapted *The Bee Season*, written by Myla Goldberg, whom she calls brilliant, and is now doing a rewrite of *Paris Under-ground*, a movie about two women who got involved in the French Resistance. And like many women writers these days, she says she in-tends to direct. The project she has in mind is called *Pilgrim's Progress* (not an adaptation of the work by John Bunyan).

Though she takes the familiar position of "less is more" in screen-writing, one quality of Foner's that still comes through in her scripts is a strong literary sensibility, a vibrant descriptive style, which of course can only be seen in the script text itself. Her script for *A*

Dangerous Woman presents a brightly specific description of a scene of a backyard party: "Japanese beetles, parrot-green cocktail napkins, and a few clear tumblers float." She also seems to be master of a subtle surprise, which has a nice shock effect on screen. For instance, in *Losing Isaiah*, instead of a scene where the white social worker Margaret (Jessica Lange in the movie) tells her husband that she wants to adopt a black baby born addicted to crack-cocaine, which would be a clichéd and obvious way to handle it, there is a conversation between Margaret and her friend Ethel, where the latter questions her motivations for wanting to do this.

And she has mastered what seems to be the central concept of filmmaking—showing rather than telling—that all veteran screenwriters have learned and seem to adhere to. In *Running on Empty*, the movie about the former radical couple on the lam and some of the repercussions of their countercultural activities, one of their sons sees a picture of them in the paper, as they were in their earlier hippie days.

Question: "Who's this?"

Answer: "Mom and Dad."

"Your job as a screenwriter," she says, "is to put in the various possibilities. So you can have a scene in a restaurant where someone will say 'I'm sorry I'm late' and the other person says 'that's O.K.' but there can be a million ways to say it's really not O.K."

One of the few women to have successfully worked in the action film genre as a writer in the modern era is Alexandra Seros, the scribe for *Point of No Return* (1993) and *The Specialist* (1994). Seros, originally from California, studied acting as part of the theater arts program at UCLA. "At some point, I found I preferred plays, and the possibility of directing. With some borrowed equipment, I made a film about the homeless, and because of that I got into the American Film Institute as a fellow. Robert Wise loved the film and I got a fellowship. Sydney Pollack would come and talk and make you feel it was possible." The writer says she is glad she tried acting first, believing it is a fine preparation for scriptwriting.

Seros, who is 53 years old (and, along with Foner, one of the few in the movie business who will admit to being more than 50 years old), credits her older brother with first getting her interested in movies. "He told me that the sets swiveled and that intrigued me. We went to see Toshiro Mifune movies. Also *Hiroshima Mon Amour* and *8½*. Even today my favorite films are *The Conversation* and *Last Tango in Paris*. In fact, they were the inspiration for *The Specialist*. I wanted to do a kind of action movie about two people who had no intimacy in their lives.

"And I love Jungian psychology. I was fascinated by the work of Eric Neuman and the shadow figure. I tried to combine Jungian psychology and dramatic theory, and tried to find an archetype, the snoop of *The Conversation*. The script just sort of went round and round. Finally I took it to the William Morris Agency, and got in touch with [industry publicist] Leslie Dart around 1986 or 1987. My agent Tom Strickler came on the scene, and I've been with him ever since."

Seros laughs, "I did have a bomb in the script, and Hollywood goes: 'Ah! A genre movie!'" She does allow, however, that her film and filmmaking theory fit well with action movies. "I like to see visual metaphors. Not a lot of dialogue. Fellini and Kurosawa worked it best. What are the images telling you? Films are visceral."

Once *The Specialist* went into production, she says, there were numerous changes in the female character, the part taken by Sharon Stone. "The woman in my version had a very different identity. But Akiva Goldman reworked the script, and made her more of a victim rather than a free agent just lacking identity."

Seros had a number of meetings with Sylvester Stallone, who played the lead in *The Specialist*. "My original concept was that his part would be a very lonely existential character. Sly said he was interested in doing that, but at the last minute reverted back to the action character."

The success of *The Specialist* assured Seros a place in the movie business. Her next big film was *Point of No Return*, a remake of Luc Bresson's *La Femme Nikita*, with Bridget Fonda in the lead. "With adaptation, you want to be true to the spirit of the original, but still have it be your own film. With your own idea, there is the freedom to start with yourself."

Seros's current favorite project, which she is pushing for development, is titled *Victory Boulevard*. "It's a kind of '*Whatever Happened to Baby Jane?*' but with over-the-hill male boxers in the lead. Three men producers came to me with the idea for the project, and I basically flipped the original Baby Jane. The problem is that the studios want younger actors for the leads."

She is also at work on a film called C.O. It's a spec script originally written for studio head Denise Donovan, optioned by DreamWorks. "It's about CIA agents. It's really *Goodfellows* for the CIA." Seros also wrote a script a few years ago—unproduced—adapted from Don DeLillo's *Libra*, the story of Lee Harvey Oswald. "But then Oliver Stone and *J.F.K.* sort of washed over us."

Seros says she prefers to have an office away from home. "My first priority is my son Bruno. But when I'm home I feel such guilt when he looks at me working that I have to get away. I have an office in the Palisades. I go to my office every day. I do very complete outlines, and once I have a good outline, I write three pages a day, go back the next day and edit that, and then write three more. And so forth."

She is not among those who feel that only a female can write certain scenes, or vice versa. "Robert Benton writes great women's roles and he's a man," she observes. "A great writer should not be using stereotypes. I strive for a real, specific male and a specific female."

Her favorite film is still Kurosawa's *The Seven Samurai*. Seros says it perfectly shows what she feels movies are best at. "I'm interested in movement and image and how they cut into our unconscious. It's the life that's lived in between the lines that makes a movie interesting. It's everything that's going on in the background."

For the straight skinny, for a historical (and somewhat different) perspective on some of these issues, it's good to go to the source. Jay Presson Allen has been in the business since the 1950s, first in television, then as the writer for luminaries such as directors Alfred Hitchcock and Sidney Lumet. Allen, who lives in Manhattan, has this advice for emerging or would-be screenwriters: "Just do it. Be lucky. And—if possible—get in on the ground floor."

Born in Texas, Allen (then Jay Presson) moved to New York to become an actress. After a brief early marriage in California, she wrote a novel, *Spring Riot*. Just after its publication in 1948 (by Rinehart), she came back to New York. Performing on radio and in cabaret, she found that acting seemed a mistake, too: "I didn't like being controlled by someone behind the footlights." Little by little, she turned to writing again, during television's "golden age," for shows such as Philco

Playhouse. And then came her play, adapted from the novel *The Prime of Miss Jean Brodie*.

During this period, Allen's novel was in the office of a literary agent. Allen says that Alfred Hitchock was in the office one day, picked it up, and after reading it made Allen an offer to go to Hollywood to write *Marnie*. Never one to give the expected answer, Allen says that she actually did not like the way *Marnie*, her first script, turned out, as much she did enjoy working with Hitchcock.

"It's flawed. But I take full responsibility for that." And she credits Hitchcock with training a first-time screenwriter. "My script was too verbose. He had to show me how to work in visual shorthand." For instance, show a bouquet of flowers in water sloshing in a honeymoon ship cabin, with a note saying congratulations, rather than having a series of scenes: wedding, trip to honeymoon suite in ship, and so on.

Unlike some current setups where a writer can be barred from a set, Allen was on hand as much as she wanted to be in the early days with Hitchcock. About the recent Writers Guild negotiations which have asked for such platforms in their contracts and a different attitude toward writers, Allen snorts: "You can't ordain respect. These things were never issues. In the main, though, I would say that it's been a very good union."

As Allen tells it, screenwriting was never something she had thought much about, nor had she pursued it either. Married by then to New York theatrical producer Lewis Allen—as she is today—she was loath then as now to go to the West Coast for work. However, "Hitchcock saw something he liked. I don't know that I would have done it for anyone else. But the chance to work with Hitch—well." Allen shrugs her shoulders as to say "that's self evident." And thus began her pattern of going to Los Angeles to work only when absolutely necessary, staying in hotels or temporary housing.

Always full of surprises, Allen says that Hitchcock, whom many have described as difficult, was a delight to work for. "He was never mean to writers. He was wonderful to writers. He was only mean to actors and, well . . . turn off your tape recorder." She said she was frequently on a Hitchcock set if she wanted to, and also could be involved in casting if she cared to be.

Allen, whose film writing career includes *Marnie* with Hitchcock and *Prince of the City* with Sidney Lumet, points out that she always worked with the top talent. She describes herself as a very fast writer, with no particular sentimental or intellectual attachment to her scripts once they are completed. In fact, she says Lumet once asked her if she was, in her words, "a little gaga. See, I couldn't remember the names of any of the characters in the script we had just finished. With me, when it's over, it's over." As an example of what she means, she says that though she did a rewrite on *The Thomas Crown Affair* after it left the pen (or the word processor) of Leslie Dixon, she doesn't remember at all what changes she made. When this interviewer expressed surprise at the news of the Dixon rewrite, Allen simply smiled, and said, "You hadn't heard?"

An offer of such work comes to her through her agent. "Do you know any writer worth their salt who doesn't have an agent?" she asks. In her case it has been the powerful agent Sam Cohen. And with even higher irony, Allen says that these days the best writing gigs are the ones that come just before the pay-or-play option is coming up: the script is done, the actors and crew have to be paid; and the movie is in trouble.

In other words, uncredited rewrites, "You do it fast, and it's for a lot of money. The best part is that you don't have to take any bloody meetings."

Allen says that in the building where she lives (which has a fancy Park Avenue address), there is frequently an empty apartment available—sometimes from friends with a *pied a terre*—that she will use to work on a project. "I simply go till I'm done," she says. "Even if that means being up all night," not requiring what other writers have described as the journeyman-like, even nine-to-five, structure they seem to need.

In the past, Allen has been quoted as saying that a director has to piss on a script a little bit in order for him [sic] to think it is his. She still stands by that quote, explaining, "It takes a controlling nature to direct a film. That's not a denigrating thing to say. It's an enormous job. If they're going to take that job, they have to feel it's theirs. That's what I meant. Anyway, if a director isn't happy with every page of that script, you're not going to get what you want anyway. The thing is to get in there and work with him. Help him define the job. That's not true in theater."

"I would never want to be a director," she says, in direct contrast with so many women writers interviewed today who claim this is the only way to maintain any control over their scripts. "When you're directing a film, it's an automatic two years out of your life," she observes. "Directing a movie is like moving an army across the country. Of course, if that's what you want to do, more power to you." Her MO—and she admitted that it might not work these days in the movie business—has always been to give priority to her personal life, her husband and daughter, to be what is referred to these days as a "stay-at-home mom," and then go to the Coast when required. "This is what you've got to do if you want to have a life. And if you want to protect yourself in some way" in order to have a personal life.

Most of her work has been adaptations, she points out, and as with other references to her work methods, she's a bit vague. "It's obvious, isn't it," she reacted upon hearing the methods of Robin Swicord, "write out the major themes in a book, find the passages that most strongly support those themes." Keeping as close to the original is what is required by the job, according to her. Producers buy a certain project, she points out, and that's what they should get given back to them.

Allen also adds that, while she has not had a prolific career, her spectrum was broad in that she managed to work in a number of different genres, though all her films have been adaptations. The reason for this she says is that she has always seen herself as a hired hand, taking the assignments given her. She makes sure to point out, however, that she almost always worked with top people.

In addition to *Marnie* in 1964 and *The Prime of Miss Jean Brodie* in 1969, her work includes *Cabaret* in 1972 (one of the few times when she wrote with a specific actor, Liza Minnelli, in mind), *Travels With My Aunt* in 1972, *40 Carats* in 1973, *Funny Lady* in 1975, *Just Tell Me What You Want* in 1980, *Prince of the City* in 1981, and *Deathtrap* in 1982 (the last three by Sidney Lumet). More recently she is credited on *Year of the Gun* in 1991 with Sharon Stone, and a western, *Liar's Poker* in 1999, along with Michael Lewis and Neil Cuthbert. Allen won screenwriting Oscars for *Cabaret* and *Prince of the City*.

Of all the films she has written, Allen's favorite is *Prince of the City*, directed by Lumet. "It turned out exactly what I had envisioned in my head," she says. "Not just what I had put on the page. Sidney never worked in Hollywood. It makes a big difference." (Meaning that he had more respect for the writer's vision, and that as a New Yorker 3,000 miles away from controlling studio executives, he pretty much did what he thought would be best for the film.)

Mixed in with her film work has been some work for television and for the stage. But like many veteran screenwriters of an earlier generation, she now prefers to do the quick and dirty work of a last minute rewrite on a feature film rather than try to play the game of working with development people. "The last time I did that," she says, "they were really young kids in development who knew nothing about films. A lot of MBAs. Really smart, but I knew I would have to spend all my time giving a tutorial, and who needs that? So I quit."

Allen does tell a humorous story "on herself," as the Irish say, about being hired by Steve McQueen to adapt an action novel he had bought for his wife, Ali MacGraw. "He was always full of games. Once we were taking a meeting with a director and a couple of producers in my hotel suite. I must have said something he didn't like about dialogue or something. Then he went into the bathroom. I smelled something burning and when I went into the bathroom I saw he had set my nightgown on fire. I put it out, came back into the room and said nothing." She laughs. "He and Ali had just been married for about a year and a half. She wanted to go back to work and he didn't really want her to, but didn't want it to appear that way. The film was never really going to get made.

"It was my first experience in trying to do an action film. Right away I could see that some of the scenes weren't very good. So I called a guy I knew—I didn't tell Steve—and asked him to do a couple action scenes for ten thousand dollars, which was a lot of money back then. When he finished, I asked the writer what was wrong with my scenes, and he said, 'You didn't kill anybody. You just lightly wounded them.' "

Though Allen is loath to take a pro forma feminist approach to women and violence, she does say, "How many ways can you blow somebody up? I don't give a shit," granting that perhaps women are just not interested in things like that.

Nor will she go very far in conjecturing about sex differences in writing style or interests. "Sure. I write differently for a man than for a woman. But that doesn't mean I can't write men's parts. You know what a male voice is, what a female voice is." Are women in general better at writing women's roles? "No. Well, maybe in some instances." Do women write differently than men? "Some do, some don't." So it goes with the blunt, but slippery, Allen.

And, as used as one is to hearing four-letter words these days, when she uses one it does pack a certain punch. Possibly it's the incongruity with her elegant Park Avenue apartment and her impeccable manners as the eighty-something gets up to offer a cheese swizzle stick, or to serve you from the silver tea service her maid has brought in.

More likely, though, it is the sense that when she uses profanity, it will be for a reason. With clear intent.

Perhaps it is this demeanor that has gotten her the reputation of someone who can be tough in meetings. Not that she likes to take them anymore. Hers is not, however, the usual stance of "they just don't make them like they used to." "Studios used to be run by moviemakers. Now they are run by business people." Not exactly a new insight, but she's thought it through.

"I've been lucky all the way around. I hit the movies at the right time for me. When they put in the development people—which is understandable by the way—everything changed. When a movie costs $20 million or $30 million, people get scared. And creative people are by definition very persuasive. They are passionate. So they put this ring of protection around executives. Kind of a 'corps de sanitaire.' But in doing this, they've lost their movie audience." She does allow, however, that "the movie business is a huge gamble. It's not like knocking out Chevrolets." And she adds that she believes that the changes in technology are so swift that no one can predict with any certainty what direction films might go in.

These days, Allen says, her preference is to do a last minute rewrite for a script that is already completed, but that may be in trouble. It also works because, in response to an impertinent question, Allen guffaws, "I'm sure I'm experiencing ageism as we speak. If they could see me, I'd probably never work at all." In fact, her white hair is perfectly coiffed, she is lightly made up, and she is wearing a below-the-knee cotton dress wth a discreetly ethnic look and sandals. It is August in Manhattan.

Sticking with her "hired hand" philosophy, Allen refuses to discuss any of the rewrites she has recently done, or what changes she made.

"Haven't a clue," she says in one of her favorite phrases to inquiries about details of work completed. "You only remember if it's contentious."

The sole exception to this is the writing she recently did for a script of *Night Witches*, about a group of valiant female fighter pilots in Russia in World War II, about half of whom were killed in combat. "I love the project. The title. The whole thing." The film will probably never get made though, because there are too many parts, and no lead. It is simply not a vehicle for any one star. (Ironically, this sounds exactly like the kind of film many feature and independent women screenwriters would love to work on.)

Allen says she never had a unique idea for a film (though her plays are of course original). This perhaps explains why she has so little sympathy for some screenwriters who complain about lack of creative control or that their scripts were changed. "That way lies madness," she proclaims. "It's a job. It's not a great creative endeavor. You get paid a great deal of money for not a lot of time. You ought to just shut up and bank it," she smiles with high irony. The only problem with trying to read Allen, of course, is that so often irony may just be the plain truth. If you can tell at all. "Where else except screenwriting can you work for such a short time and make so much money?" she asks rhetorically.

Surprisingly, these veteran screenwriters have differing thoughts about women's special proclivity for scriptwriting. Naomi Foner has said that women don't really write any differently than men do, but they may have a more "cooperative" character. Alexandra Seros sees no difference at all between women and men's writings; Allen is the most quixotic. "Some [women writers] do [write differently from men]. Some don't."

Most of these professionals of long duration seem to have come into the business either through an already established personal connection (like Mathison) or, in the case of Elaine May and Jay Presson Allen, by having a strong reputation in another field and attracting attention that way. In a way, they were already celebrities.

You might say that Naomi Foner, like Mathison, "married in." Yet Foner's first scripts were written because she was already in that type of work environment. And she is surely not the first woman in any field to merge her career interests to those of her spouse. A more interesting take on Foner is her longevity and her openness about many aspects of the business. Recently she said that she sort of went underground when she turned 50, feeling her usefulness in the movie business was nil. But she had a change of heart, threw herself a latter-day birthday party, and decided to get back to work.

Only one of these screenwriters, Alexandra Seros, approached her career the way other women screenwriters do today: by going to school, finding a mentor, and taking it from there. In this way, she is perhaps predictive of the current crop of "hot" women screenwriters.

Chapter Three

The New Professionals

In their insistence on professionalism, on getting paid top dollar for top work, the first wave of veteran screenwriters paved the way for the new professionals. Some writers who have benefited might be termed the next wave, or the new professionals: Gina Wendkos, who wrote *Jersey Girl*, *Coyote Ugly*, *The Princess Diaries*, and *The Perfect Man*; Leslie Dixon, who wrote *Outrageous Fortune*, *The Thomas Crown Affair*, and *Pay It Forward*; and Audrey Wells, who wrote *The Truth About Cats and Dogs*, *Guinevere*, and *Under the Tuscan Sun*.

Another recent stellar example is the success of Sofia Coppola with her Oscar win for *Lost in Translation*, only her second feature (*The Virgin Suicides* was her first). In 2004, a year in which every other major award went to the epic *Lord of the Rings*, her win for a relatively small, personal film is perhaps even more extraordinary.

Questions about Coppola's entry into the business don't really apply, as clearly her whole life and heritage have been training for such a career. More pertinent is seeing what subjects she is attracted to, the shape her films take, and her work methods.

Her first film, *The Virgin Suicides* (2000), is not only about women, but about sisters, taking up an important female issue of the time: teenage suicide. Her second film, *Lost in Translation*, is precisely the kind of script you would not expect from the daughter of filmmaker Francis Ford Coppola, whose major successes have been in the epic mode. As Sofia told me, "My script has lots of spaces and holes. It was based on taking notes of different little impressions. Little stories I'd thought about over the years, and collected in notebooks, and then I started collecting pictures of the visuals." The emotional impact of this kind of intimate, small film has led some critics to wonder if the new ascendancy of female filmmakers will turn the tide from the huge action-packed blockbuster movies that are the province of male filmmakers.

While Coppola has no direct comment on this, she does say, "I definitely have had friendships and moments with people from different backgrounds and in different stages of their lives. Brief encounters where you know someone for a few days and it seems you've had a whole lifetime, and it shapes who you are as a person. To me that's like the most comforting or best thing in life, when you have a little connection or you both find something funny, and it makes you feel not alone. And I like movies that just meander along, where it's more about the feelings. I was just compiling all these different things that I liked and hoped that it would all add up to the feeling I wanted to give in *Lost in Translation*."

She also says that she wrote her script with Bill Murray in mind. Another deliberate choice was setting the film in Tokyo, a place she had visited for long periods of time and that made her feel that one day she would like to make a movie there. "A friend of mine was doing a fashion show in Tokyo and asked me to come help produce it. While I was there I met someone on a magazine who asked me to do photos. While I was working as a photographer, I found Tokyo to be an interesting and stimulating place to work."

Coppola studied painting at the California Institute for the Arts, and before deciding to become a full-time writer-director, worked as a photographer (in Japan) and also had her own clothing business. But eventually and perhaps inevitably she was drawn to moviemaking. Her very first movie, *Lick the Star*, premiered at the Venice Film Festival. You're tempted to say "nothing like starting at the top," but Coppola is neither defensive nor braggy about her heritage. "Surely there is the possibility that maybe I got some kind of filmmaking gene," she says, "but it's definitely not easy. It's hard and scary work to write something personal and then take it round trying to get financing. It was hard to shoot this in 27 days. People can think whatever they want."

Lost in Translation is an original script, and some have noted the similarity to *Brief Encounter*, the 1946 movie directed by David Lean about two middle-age married people—Celia Johnson and Trevor Howard—who are attracted to each other but are committed elsewhere. Coppola disarms this "homage" by herself, using the phrase brief encounter now and again while discussing her movie. By contrast, her film *The Virgin Suicides* was strictly an adaptation. In both cases, however, her attraction to her subjects have been highly personal. For example, she fell in love with Jeffrey Eugenides's novel, *The Virgin Suicides*. "When I read the book, it became one of my favorites," she says.

I loved how the story had serious and tragic sides, but was also funny. You know how you get about those books that you love—"Oh, they're going to make a movie of it! Are they going to do it right?" I had those feelings, and then I heard a little about how [others] were doing it, and I got the feeling it wasn't going to be treated as delicately as I thought the book deserved. I became protective of it and I started thinking, "Oh, the film should open like this, not like that," and so I thought I'd start writing it down, instead of talking about it. I started writing a couple scenes, and then I got into it. I was doing it on the weekends. I thought, "Oh, I'll just do one more scene. If nothing else, I'll learn how to adapt a book into a screenplay."

From the opposite end of the geographic and economic spectrum, Gina Wendkos is a screenwriter who has managed to move into the mainstream as a successful writer. Irreverent and witty, short and with nice blue eyes, Wendkos hails from the New York borough of Queens, and studied art in colleges in Maryland and Pennsylvania. Drawn to performance art, she supported herself as a bartender and waitress while performing and writing plays in Manhattan, mainly at the American Place Theater. She also worked as a copywriter, and even wrote mini-scripts for women answering sex, or talk radio. According to columnist Jason Gay from the *New York Observer*, "Ms. Wendkos said she has long been fascinated with call girls, ever since she was in her early 20s and struggling to make it as a writer in Manhattan. One of her first jobs was writing little scripts for the women who answered

976 phone lines, 'I just had to write my imagination. You know, like *Put your hand there.*'" Ms. Wendkos also worked extensively in theater and performing art, where, she said, she encountered a number of women who were professionally hustling on their side. "It was interesting to see their lives and the different belief systems they had from civilians . . . the different rationales some of them used, and the different attitudes they had about sex and men and money."[1]

When one of her plays did well, it was staged in L.A., at the Odyssey Theater. And when the *Los Angeles Times* gave it a rave review, she says, "The agents came around and I fell into sitcoms."

After seven years writing for television—*Hooperman, Private Eye,* and *Wiseguy*—Wendkos said she became bored and decided to try her hand at features. She says this came about mainly through the generosity of the producer Jerry Bruckheimer and Chad Oman, the president of Bruckheimer Productions. She started with the script for *Jersey Girl* and then wrote *Coyote Ugly.*

She laughs at some of the hoopla surrounding *Coyote Ugly* (2000), which was based on an article in GQ magazine about the same-titled bar in Manhattan and its sexy cocktail waitresses. "Bruckheimer bought the article," Wendkos says, deciding that she was the perfect writer for the film, having spent a great deal of time working in bars. But some women's groups complained that the movie treated women as sex objects. Wendkos laughs this off: "I don't think *Coyote Ugly* was that important to make such a big feminist fuss over. It was just a little film. But if they wanted to do that, I would defend it."

"Just put late thirties," Wendkos instructed me when I spoke with her during a work break, in her home office. "Writers are essentially loners," she says. "That's why I don't mind working alone, or being alone. If I want company, I just research things on the Internet or play with TiVo. That's what I do when I get stuck writing. Or I read a book. But I'm working the whole time, really."

Wendkos says she has no desire to direct. "Sure. It's a way to protect your property, but once you turn it in, that's pretty much that. You can't control it beyond that. Sometimes I get angry at changes made but there's nothing you can do about it."

She also has a unique take about being on a movie set, which so many writers and the Writers Guild have asked about, "It's boring really. I was never barred from a set or anything. But there's a lot of waiting around. You try to act busy, but you end up hanging about, getting in people's way, and eating too much from the food cart."

Her advice to beginning screenwriters is, "Just do it. Go into a room alone and shut the door. And write about something you care about.

"You have to have an ear. You can sharpen your ear. But first you must have a gift for storytelling. It's like being a gymnast. If you don't have the original bodybuilding skills, it won't help. Writing is like that. It's about what's underneath. I don't even know what it is." Wendkos adds, "I follow the character. It's an intuitive thing." And she says that she does not believe in scriptwriting classes or the many seminars given around the country that promise to make you a screenwriter in a few weeks. "Only lawyers take those classes," says Wendkos. "I guess because they write briefs all day they think they are writers."

Nor does she think that women have any special abilities in writing for other women. But she does see certain other sex differences. "Men can write characters just as well as women," she asserts. "But they can write action better. Men know how to construct a story—how to make an elevator crash. I think women don't see the world in a mechanical way. That's why men seem to be drawn to action films. They have a more natural ability to understand the sequence of action in a movie."

Nevertheless, Wendkos has been hired for movies with big women's roles. Most recently, there is her script for *The Princess Diaries*, with its role for an older woman (Julie Andrews as a grandmother) as well as the ingénue (Anne Hathaway as the princess). And she is credited with the idea for the sequel. "It's a Cinderella story, really. As for doing the story for the second film, that was in my contract. If your agent is any good, it's written in."

These brusque observations somewhat set you up for her startling comment on women in the movie business in California: "Most have gone to the same, the right colleges, and know each other through that. The truth is no woman in the film industry ever did anything for my career. In fact, the only two times I was betrayed out here it was by a woman. Amy Pascal is fabulous. A few others. And the women in the theater in New York were gracious and generous to me, especially my mentor, Julia Miles, at the American Place Theater.

"I love California. But most of the women in the industry here are just bitches in Prada."

Wendkos is married, with two stepsons.

Leslie Dixon is another woman writer who has managed to move into permanent mainstream writing status. A tiny, seemingly unassuming woman, her most recent hits are *Freaky Friday*, *Pay It Forward*, and—a few years ago—*Mrs. Doubtfire*. A native of northern California, and the granddaughter (on different sides of her family) of photographer Dorothea Lange and painter Maynard Dixon, Dixon nevertheless says, in a humorous way, that she does not believe being visual is a particular quality of hers. In fact she is in general quite self-critical, saying her early scripts were far too wordy, a common complaint about beginning screenwriters.

The details of Dixon's career rise are relatively well known to those in movie circles. A native San Franciscan, she moved to Los Angeles when she realized she wanted to write scripts, and worked at various office jobs while immersing herself in writing and figuring out what kind of films were selling. Her breakthrough was fairly rapid, yet she has said that every time she starts to feel good about her progress, or high on herself, she just looks up on her wall and sees a picture of her grandmother, Dorothea Lange. "And when I see that picture, I say to myself, 'Get over yourself.' "

With a refreshing directness, Dixon told me her criterion for a successful script: "How many job offers you get after it's finished."

There were apparently quite a few after the 1986 hit *Outrageous Fortune*, which she wrote for Shelley Long and Bette Midler. Dixon has written with Midler in mind a number of times and admires her a great deal: "Bette is incredibly gifted, of course, but she's also very honest, very generous. The best part is that she did it all herself. She came from nothing." Dixon says the original idea for *Outrageous Fortune* came from a man, Robert Cort of Interscope Films, who felt that the market was ripe for a female buddy film and asked Dixon to come up with a script. The highly acclaimed *Thelma and Louise*, which usually gets all the credit for this, was made five years later, proving one of Dixon's ideas, that comedies are not high on the list of prestige projects in the movie business. *Outrageous Fortune* was a moderate financial success, with mainly positive reviews. Yet while Dixon says she worked hard to emphasize female friendship in her script, it was not until 2004 that the movie gained status as the first comic female buddy film, and received that billing in art houses and women in film retrospectives.

Dixon describes herself as taking a very practical, even pragmatic approach to the business of screenwriting. And her game plan has worked. For instance, trying to avoid the perhaps permanent slot of being a comedy writer, she did what most scriptwriters abhor and few established writers will undertake: the dreaded "spec script," one written with no advance money or guarantee that it will be made into a film, on speculation.

Dixon went after a thriller, *The Thomas Crown Affair.*

Though it was a remake of the 1967 film and therefore had some potential preconceptions to overcome, *Thomas Crown* was a huge critical and commercial success. And while Dixon says it was not necessarily her intent, the movie found favor with feminists for its two progressive and multifaceted roles for women: the wise woman played by Faye Dunaway in the part of Thomas Crown's therapist, a deliberate homage by Dixon to Dunaway's role in the original film. And there is the romantic lead, an accomplished professional woman in her forties, played by René Russo.

Yet Dixon says that the most intriguing and challenging roles to write were actually those of the men in the movie, mentioning in particular the part of the cop (Dennis Leary, who did bring many layers to an already multidimensional character).

Dixon does not pull any punches in discussing the travails of working within today's studio system and its corporate culture. She says, for instance, she tried to hold out for a more sophisticated plot structure, and a conclusion where the male and female leads in *The Thomas Crown Affair* do not end up together. But this story line was rejected by the studio.

She is as blunt in talking about her highly successful film *Pay It Forward* (2000). "I'm always in support of a movie when it is being made and marketed," she says. "I never interfere with the promotion of a film, and would never sabotage the movie in any way while it is out there. But," she asks rhetorically, "after the project is over, what difference can it make?" (I can attest to her support of a project. On a press junket for *Outrageous Fortune*, the then 26-year-old Dixon was chipper and enthusiastic about every aspect of the movie, and in fact her very presence was unique. Screenwriters as a rule do not turn up on the interview circuit.)

Today, Dixon does not hesitate to say, "It's dangerous to get an actor just off an Oscar. No one ever says the "N" word [meaning "no"]. And in *Pay It Forward* there were two Oscar winners: Kevin Spacey and Helen Hunt. If one wanted a long speech, the other would want one of similar length. They each wanted child abuse in their backstory, and a monologue about it. I tried to talk them out of it. Two such speeches were just too much. However. . . ."

She also says that "the movie really should have ended when story line 'A' did—that is, when boy gets girl. But again an edict came down, and the movie did not end there, but with the death of the young boy played by Haley Joel Osment, the kind of sappy ending the film has now." (Dixon also made a similar comment about actors' egos out of control in *The Next Best Thing*, the movie with Madonna and Rupert Everett. Dixon produced the film, which was written by her husband, Tom Ropelewski.)

Of her work on *Mrs. Doubtfire*, a 1993 film with which she is credited, Dixon says that the film was actually a rewrite. "I put in little bits that I thought would appeal to Robin Williams. Kind of like offering a piece of bait. Scripts are often written for a star this way." She says her method for writing Williams's part was to think of several different women (Williams's character cross-dresses in order to be near his children, who have been separated from him by divorce).

While Dixon seems proud of *Mrs. Doubtfire*, *That Old Feeling*, which she wrote in 1997, and which stars Bette Midler, did not turn out exactly the way she wanted, Dixon says. She feels the same way about *Big Business*, the comedy starring Bette Midler and Lily Tomlin. Both films were rewrites.

Though she does have high praise for Bette Midler, she believes there is no comic actress comparable to Goldie Hawn, who starred in Dixon's script for *Overboard*. "Perhaps the closest would be Sandra Bullock. But it's very hard to do comedy, and in general directors and studios shy away from it. With comedy, if you fail it's an ignominious defeat. Besides," she laughs, "You ain't [*sic*] going to get an Oscar writing a comedy."

When I spoke with Dixon she was between projects. But she warned that once she commits to a script, she is generally inaccessible. In fact her answering machine message is a chipper, "This is Leslie, fabulously unavailable." This may strike the right tone of bravado with industry insiders; in person however Dixon seemed open, even vulnerable. And when I called her a few months later for fact verification and a photo request, Dixon answered her own phone with a quick "hello." Surprised to get her on the phone so easily, when I remarked about her lack of an assistant, she replied that it was "good for her" to do her own secretarial work, and for errand running there was always the nanny.

Disarmingly, Dixon said that very few women in the movie business have actually helped her. "I go to all these 'women and film' events in Hollywood, and I look around the room, and I don't see one woman who has done anything for me, or for that matter for any other woman in the business either."

If Naomi Foner came up in what might be called a golden or even platinum time of free-form films of the 1970s, and Jay Presson Allen got in on the ground floor, today's more businesslike, even removed, attitude can be seen in the work and approach of a writer (and hopeful writer-director) such as Audrey Wells.

Another consummate professional, though one who is a bit more guarded, Wells is described by Gina Wendkos as a current "darling of Disney." Wells lets no ball drop, taking four "call waitings" during our interview in case the call might be from her producer, putting into practice the well-known dictum that Los Angeles is a town built on relationships.

At the time of the interview, Wells had just completed a script for Imagine Entertainment, the company of Brian Grazer and Ron Howard. "If you mention it, please do mention my cowriter, Will Richter," she requested, going on to describe the film, tentatively called *Golden Gate*, as chronicling the rise of San Francisco. There is no opening date as yet, and she reminds the interviewer that—while she hopes this doesn't happen—not all films get made.

The soft-spoken Wells, with dark hair and fair skin, is originally from Northern California and a Berkeley graduate with a degree in communications. After moving to Los Angeles, she picked up an MFA in film production from UCLA. But her first "real" job was writing for various media outlets for Democratic political campaigns. The first career passion of her life, however, was for jazz. In fact, Wells is still miffed at a mention on the Internet Movie Database that she once fibbed to get a job as a disc jockey.

While working for the Corporation for Public Broadcasting and traveling for her job to Alaska, Wells wrote her first script, "Radio Free Alaska." She gave it to Tyler Benser, a lifelong friend in the movie business, who gave it to an agent. "It was hip pocketed," she observes, meaning that the agent was under no obligation to actively place it. But the script did sell, to Paramount, in 1989. So the importance of an agent comes up again.

Wells's next big project was for David Geffen: a movie about a female campaign manager. That film did not get made, and Wells did a number of rewrites for other scripts around this time. (According to Joan Tewkesbury, the list of approved "script doctors" is so short that one inevitably is rewriting the work of a friend.)

Wells's breakthrough film was *The Truth About Cats and Dogs*, a surprise hit for both her and Miramax. It had been a negative pickup, she says, meaning that the film had already been completed, and Miramax bought the negative. Even so, Wells says there were a number of changes she regrets in a film that is nevertheless quite progressive in its women's roles. For instance, in her original script, both the glamorous blonde, played by Uma Thurman, and the "dumpy" brunette, Janeane Garofalo, sleep with the hero, but their friendship survives this acid test. In the film as it turned out, Thurman only flirts with him.

In her first draft, Well says, the "dumb blonde" had a better sense of her worth as a commodity, perceiving that her attractiveness and "marketability" were limited by time. She is shrewd as well as cute. In the actual film, Uma Thurman is instead a fantasized love object in the category of a ditzy, if pleasant enough, blonde. Wells seems to be actively working toward a positive representation of female friendship on film, something she achieved fully in *Under the Tuscan Sun*.

Perhaps the film's most original sequence—and as of this writing there is really no other like it—is the scene of phone sex/mutual masturbation between Garofalo and Ben Chaplin, playing the film's hero. (The phone sex scene, for instance, where Jennifer Jason Leigh makes household money to help support her family by doing phone sex for hire in Altman's *Short Cuts* is, after all, "just business.") According to Wells, the bit actually contemporized a "Cyrano de Bergerac" type scenario: in this case it is a male hero who has a romantic fantasy about someone who is not the person he thinks she is. In *Cats and Dogs*, it is not Thurman who is on the phone with Chaplin, but Garofalo; in *Cyrano* it is he who has written the letters, not who Roxanne thinks wrote the letters.

Though *Cats and Dogs* was a career turning point for Wells, she says she was not that pleased with the way Miramax distributed the movie or handled the publicity. Still, this film raised industry awareness of Wells's work and brought her a wider circle of contacts. Wells followed this film with *The Kid* with Bruce Willis, *Guinevere* (which she also directed) with Stephen Rea, and *George of the Jungle*. Of all of these, Wells says that the children's film *George of the Jungle* ended up being the one closest to her original concept.

Wells says she wrote Disney's *The Kid* with Bruce Willis in mind. That tactic worked, and Willis took the part of a curmudgeon who discovers he has a heart after all. Discounting possible references to *Big* with Tom Hanks, or *Back to the Future* with its time travel scenes, Wells says her inspiration for *The Kid* was *A Christmas Carol* by Dickens.

Guinevere, though it did eventually get widely and generally well reviewed, was still one of her most difficult movies to get off the ground. "It was a huge struggle," she says. Wells managed to find a distributor, Valenium, only after she took the movie to the Sundance Film Festival. *Guinevere* is about a middle-aged man's affairs with much younger women. "What do you have against dating women your own age?" asks the mother of one of the young women. Wells seems intent on creating and emphasizing roles for women of all ages, and even making a didactic point or two.

Cleverly sidestepping the question of whether it takes a woman to write a woman's part, Wells says that her general approach to writing a script is to identify most with the underdog. "My scripts are about the process of healing, of moving a character away from a position of pain." More often than not, she observes, in our society the underdog is a woman.

Wells says she decided to direct for two simple reasons: "Writing can be very lonely, and directing is more fun. When you direct you can hire brilliant people to carry weights around for you. So . . . it's not just you."

When she is writing, Wells says her schedule is usually to do nothing for six weeks, hate herself for the next three, and then write for the last six. "Somehow I can back time it. But now that I have a baby, procrastination is no longer a luxury I can afford," she explains.

Wells is a strong supporter of a writer's control over a script, its casting and the right to be on a set while a film is being made. In the case of *The Truth About Cats and Dogs*, *The Kid*, and *Guinevere*, she was part of the casting decisions. "But the truth is, it's a director's medium," she observes. "And if you don't get along with the director you're not going to have much of an impact, no matter what."

Her most recent success is *Under the Tuscan Sun*. Opening to generally good reviews and praise for Wells's ability to insert narrative into the journal by Frances Mayes, which chronicles the story of a house being refurbished in Italy, the movie makes clear that Wells is working hard at writing enlightened women's roles, though she also says she worked hard on other aspects of the script. "I opened up the book both in structure and in theme," says Wells.

The heroine (Diane Lane) is a professional woman whose closest personal relationship is with her lesbian friend Patti (Sandra Oh). After a divorce, the Lane character's sexual adventures are chronicled with nonjudgemental clarity, and neither guilt nor affirmation. The movement toward happy independence that is the arc of the film, even with its inevitable Hollywood happy ending, is very different from the book in which the writer/narrator actually has a male partner throughout, and there is no emotional journey. Instead, the driving force for partnership in this film, and it is not a sexual one, comes from a friend—a clever and loyal lesbian.

This extremely positive image is an original Wells addition, and is in no part of the original book. (Some might cynically observe, though, that many powerful lesbians now "run" Hollywood, or part of it, and this depiction could only have helped Wells's career.) In fact, as wonderful as Diane Lane is in the film, she doesn't get all the best lines of dialogue. "Can you star 69 Italy?" asks Patti, when trying to get in touch with her dear friend.

One thing becomes clear from talking to the new professionals, whether or not you like their work or them or have mixed feelings: They have—to a woman—accommodated themselves to the demands of the times. Wells says, "You can do as much as possible to help the role of women or the underdog. I try this in all my films. But you have to be clever enough to get these images through without upsetting any studio preconceptions." Dixon had a similar thought. "You can be as breakthrough as you want, as I was with *Outrageous Fortune* and in insisting on working on a comedy. But ultimately the big decisions come from the big egos you're writing for, or the big egos above you."

And none of these women writers, oddly enough, have had the experience of being helped by another woman. This makes a fascinating comparison with what Frances Marion told interviewer DeWitt Bodeen in 1969: "Too many women go around these days saying women in important positions don't help their own sex, but that was never my experience. In my case there were Marie Dressler, Lois Weber, Mary Pickford, Elsie Janis, Mary Roberts Rinehart, Adela Rogers St. Johns, Hedda Hooper, Bess Meredyth, Anita Loos, Ella Wheeler Wilcox who encouraged me."[2]

Both Leslie Dixon and Gina Wendkos have forthrightly declared that no film industry woman helped them at all, and Coppola and Wells came up, respectively, through family and other connections. Still, they all see their craft as a profession, whatever their point of entry, and whether they are working on a mass appeal, or a personal film.

Chapter Four

Breakaway Queens and Genre Benders: Women Writers Stretching and Bending the Film Form

A potent antidote to the formulaic, bland, and predictable industry feature films that some women screenwriters and cineastes have complained about (even as some struggled to get hired) are movies written by women who have pushed at, in some cases changed, the form of their films.

Some notable writers who have successful managed this are Barbara Turner, who most memorably wrote *Pollock*, as well as the features *Petulia* and *Georgia*, and television movies including *The War Between the Tates*; Lynn Hershmann Leeson who wrote *Conceiving Ada*; and Sally Potter who wrote (and directed) *Orlando* and *The Tango Lesson*. Possibly a more familiar name is that of Callie Khouri, who wrote the giant genre-killer *Thelma and Louise*, directed by Ridley Scott.

Orlando (1993), for instance, is adapted from the Virginia Woolf novel with a timeline moving from the Renaissance to the twentieth century. It stars Tilda Swinton as the protagonist who starts out as a young male nobleman and changes sex over the centuries to become a contemporary female. It is clearly a movie that is not going to be geared to the popular taste, though if you know the work of British filmmaker Sally Potter, it is not a big surprise, for she has always insisted on the freedom to make movies which please her.

Yet some of these films have reached a wider audience, by hook or by crook. Though few expected it, *Pollock* was nominated for two major categories: Best Actor (Ed Harris, who also directed it) and Best Supporting Actress (Marcia Gay Harden).

Barbara Turner wrote the film. In fact, she has made a name for herself in the movie writing business by writing films with a distinct female sensibility, whether or not this was a conscious choice. *Petulia,* starring Julie Christie, stunningly captured the zeitgeist of the late 1970s, and was, as *New Yorker* critic Penelope Gilliatt was the first to see at the time, clearly and obviously a portrait of its era. It also provided a picture of a fragmented female, played with appropriate angst by Christie. It even has a prescient theme of spousal abuse. Petulia is beat up by her beautiful and wealthy young husband (Richard Chamberlain); she sporadically but inconclusively turns to a sympathetic doctor (George C. Scott) for emotional support. Turner is also the scriptwriter for another female-titled and -centered film, *Georgia,* written for her daughter Jennifer Jason Leigh (Leigh coscripted and directed her own film, *Anniversary Party,* in 2001).

Turner says that she originally got into the scriptwriting business as a means of supporting her acting, and that eventually the scriptwriting took over the acting. In her early Hollywood days, Turner was married to the actor Vic Morrow; Leigh is their daughter. "After I'd been doing it for awhile," she says, "I realized that I really was a writer and not an actress, if writing was the way I was making my living."

It is also to Turner we must turn in appreciation for the creation of the part that resulted in an Oscar for Marcia Gay Harden: a dark horse nomination, a sleeper win. And a great part for a woman in a movie about a man. To write this role, Turner had to come up with a nearly impossible screen character, though obviously she existed in real life: a woman who sacrificed her own talent to that of "her man," who is strong and vocal at times to the point of being obnoxious, yet who in no way loses her self-respect or ours. In our sometimes conflicted postfeminist world where an occasional feminazi would inevitably be in the audience for a film such as *Pollock,* this is quite an achievement, to take nothing away from Harden's performance as Pollock's lover-then-wife Lee Krasner. "Lee was very tough on him in real life," observes Turner. "And she kept people away from Pollock [in the sense of protecting him.]"

So here are at least three great women's roles: Petulia, Georgia, and Lee Krasner.

The chronologically first of these, in the film *Petulia,* has a structure that matches the splintery 1970s: a crazy quilt of forward-moving cross-cutting which perfectly captures Petulia's confusion, especially her inability to commit.[1] Scenes move from the affluent couchings of her marriage, to the doctor's office, to a hastily thrown together marital trip to Mexico. "With *Petulia*," she says, "I knew the novelist, John Haase. We worked together on the script. The structure was to flash forward. It was the only way to encompass the novel."

An even more extreme example of this free-ranging, crosscutting style, which Turner has developed, can be seen in the original script for *Pollock*, based on the book *Jackson Pollock: An American Saga* by Steven Naifeh and Gregory White Smith. Speaking from her home office in California, Turner said that she got the assignment for the film from Ed Harris, who was considering a number of different writers, because he liked her pitch.

"My pitch was that I would write a script that would mirror a Pollock work of art."

In fact, the script Turner turned in to Harris begins in 1916, in Phoenix, Arizona, where the real life Jackson Pollock was born. After one page it forwards to 1950, then to 1952, and then the Long Island home Pollock and Lee Krasner had together. At this point it moves back to 1916 and back and forth a few more times. On page 5 the script moves to 1941, and then on page 14 to 1937. Though it primarily stays in the 1950s, altogether there are twenty-nine changes in time and place.

This structure would seem in some ways (despite the chronologically "correct" start of the script) congruent with Turner's statement about her intent for the film, yet in fact this is not the way the movie turned out. "I was in shock," says Turner about her reaction to the movie when she first saw the finished product. "It was very strange when I did see it. I told Jennifer [Jason Leigh] to come with me 'cause I had a feeling I would be in for a big surprise." The actual film opens with a scene in the 1940s, showing Jackson Pollock with his brother and sister-in-law in an apartment in New York. Krasner is in the scene too, and it ends with Pollock getting emotionally out of control.

After that beginning, which is tucked further along in the final draft of the screenplay, the movie proceeds more or less chronologically, with some explanatory flashbacks. As Ed Harris has shaped the film, *Pollock* is one giant flashback, not the rapidly cut juxtaposition of chronologically out of order scenes—some short, some long—which sprinkle Turner's original script.

POLLOCK
I can't do it. I'm not going to be able to do it.

SANDE
Yeah you can. Pull yourself together.
We'll get you through . . .

INT. LEE'S STUDIO

Jackson's sound asleep in bed. His filthy clothes are tumbled on the floor. Fresh clothes lie across the back of a chair.

Lee withdraws milk and eggs from the grocery bag . . . pours milk into a glass, cracks two or three eggs into it.

INT. EIGHTH STREET APT.—NIGHT

STELLA POLLOCK's large, handsome—a mythic mother figure, all loving acceptance. The pride in her sons shines on her face.

STELLA
(Jackson's smile; Jackson's reticent privacy)
Jack, you look grand.

POLLOCK
It's swell you're here.

She embraces him.

STELLA
Sande tells me how well you're doing . . .

INT. HALLWAY—EIGHTH ST. APT.—Evening

MUSIC BLASTS double echo—Benny Goodman's "Sing Sing Sing" fairly shakes the building. The jungle drum solo pours into the stairwell.

INT. JACKSON'S STUDIO

The five are at the drop-leaf table. There's the usual gallon of cheap red wine in the center of it. Stella's prepared a feast out of nothing.

                              LEE
        (re the jazz)
        Are you sure you can hear that, Jackson?

Everyone else ignores the blasting sound. Stella's impossible to read. She's like an American Indian woman—immobile, inscrutable. The relationship between her and Jackson is very taut, everything understood between them without talking. Like two cats sitting next to each other . . . close, but not engaged.

But unlike most industry writers who either heap lavish praise on their fellow moviemakers or else disavow the final film version entirely, bitterly complaining about the loss of control over their original work, Turner still has praise and high regard for director/star Ed Harris.

"This [her M.O.] is what I did with *Pollock*," she details. "I read about his life and looked at his paintings. I really tried to study his life and my script had more interaction with Pollock's real-life peers.

"As the movie turned out, it's more book-ended. It's a flashback. And Ed made it much more personal.

"It was strange when he invited me to see it. It is what I wrote and it isn't what I wrote. Ed made the film he had to make, but I was a little stunned."

She went on to say that she got over her initial shock, well enough that she plans to work with Harris again. But that she still feels her script was more in synch with the way Pollock the man and artist really was: freer, looser.

Turner says that she was originally hired by one of the movie's producers, James Francis Trezza, who was working for Harris. At the time, Turner says, Trezza was only 19 years old. Her first draft was some 260 pages long, from an 800-page book, and she was just finishing the movie *Georgia* when *Pollock* was being made. According to Turner, there were numerous drafts.

As is well-known, Turner says that Harris put a great deal of his own money, time, and energy into the project, which he had in the hopper for many years. And while she is public about her initially ambivalent reactions to seeing *Pollock*, her next project will be to work on a novel Harris bought for his wife Amy Madigan. "It's by a wonderful new novelist named A. L. Kennedy."

Turner says she likes to work on adaptations because there is something to work from. "I see myself more as an interpreter than a creator. I try to make myself as invisible as possible. 'Cause I don't do outlines. Instead, I try to service the writer. If it ain't broke don't fix it. I try to stay out of the way of the work."

In fact, she said that the only piece of advice that she gave to her daughter (one of three) when Jennifer Jason Leigh decided to cowrite and direct her first feature was "less words."

Still, the screenplay for *Pollock* that Turner loaned me has a number of beautiful, very "literary" scene instructions, and some pointed character observations. For instance, though it is not a scene that made it into the final cut for the feature, there are specific descriptions of the young Pollock brothers which are almost lyric in their sweep:

Twenty acres of parched Arizona farmland with its irrigation ditches. Chickens wander aimlessly. Three iron bedsteads are given some cool under the branches of the umbrella tree. The hot wind sends dawn into incredible shades of pink, orange and purple.

The CAMERA PANS over some few feet to FIVE TOWHEADED POLLOCK BOYS, backs to CAMERA, buck naked . . . just pulled off sheets and out of bed, fallen into an unformed line, hands on hips, barely awake . . . skinny, healthy boy bodies, the stance variations of and in deference to fourteen-year-old CHARLES, the eldest.

Turner says this description came from the book on which the script is based, the book which Ed Harris's father sent to him, because his father saw so many physical similarities between his son the actor and Pollock. She says she found the Arizona daybreak scene in the novel irresistible: "The five Pollock brothers used to sleep outside in summer. I thought it was a beautiful image of the five of them at dawn; and the dog, too, a very important part of their lives."

And in fact including that scene in the final film would have elucidated the beginning of *Pollock*, which is a bit confusing if you don't know much about the artist's life. For the movie as it starts uses the scene where the adult Jackson Pollock is seen with Krasner, his brother and his brother's wife. Unless you know about Pollock, the relationship among these people is quite confusing, and not the attention-getter it was probably intended to be.

Other unusual or quirky bits in Turner's script include the description of Peggy Guggenheim (Amy Madigan), Pollock's patron. Turner makes sure to have included the description of Peggy Guggenheim as wearing white anklets and having hairy legs, a nicely specific and identifying bit. This, she says, came from the book on which the movie is based, and it is found in many recorded descriptions of Peggy Guggenheim. "I wouldn't make that up," Turner laughs. "I think that might be libelous."

And though it is not a hallmark of Turner as a dialogue writer, she has picked up on a figure of speech that both Pollock and Lee Krasner use throughout the movie: "No three ways about it." Written like this, in prosaic prose, it doesn't seem so extraordinary. Yet this piece of dialogue is one way of presenting a bonding between the two, and some signal indicating their unique, private, shared, and—most importantly—out of kilter, offslant view of the world. In doing research for the film, Turner says she had noticed that Krasner used that phrase in some documentary footage, and decided to make good use of it in the script.

Turner is originally from Brooklyn, studied acting at the University of Texas for a year, and then came back to New York. Her older brother had been in Texas, and "he was supposed to keep an eye on me." (In fact she liked Austin well enough that she wanted it as the setting for *Georgia*, but in the end, at the suggestion of daughter Jennifer, the film was set in Seattle.) She moved to California at the invitation of her then-boyfriend, actor Vic Morrow, and pursued her acting career there until eventually writing took over. "I got out to Hollywood because Vic was going to be in *Blackboard Jungle* and he said 'C'mon out.' I did." (Morrow died of a terrible accident during the filming of John Landis's *The Twilight Zone* in 1982 along with two Vietnamese children, one of whom he heroically tried to rescue. Union work rules were adjusted after this event.)

Turner's scriptwriting, originally undertaken by her as a dare, was at first a means of supporting herself and her family, as she and Morrow struggled as actors. They even cowrote an adaptation of the Jean Genet play, *Deathwatch*, which Morrow directed. *Petulia* was made in 1968, but most of Turner's writing in the 1970s and 1980s was for television movies: *Eye of the Sparrow, Sessions, Freedom, The War Between the Tates, The Dark Side of Innocence*, and *The Affair*.

Though some writers have found television work less frustrating because it's more hands-on (and therefore more communal, or so goes the reasoning), Turner says she feels the opposite: "I found TV even worse. So many hands in. Everything gets homogenized. Unless you have a really strong producer."

Like many writers, Turner says that being a producer on her own film is the best way to go, and this was born out by her experience with *Georgia*. "The idea was really from Jennifer. A two-sentence idea, which was to follow two sisters. One has talent, one doesn't. But the second sister sort of heats up the first. Jennifer has known Mare [Winningham, who plays one of the sisters] for years and wanted her for the film, so that was one easy decision." Turner also said that some of her research for the movie came from having watched her own three daughters growing up, and their interactions.

Georgia had been written for a couple years, she said, before Leigh sold the film at Cannes. "The amazing thing about Jennifer is that you're really free to work. There's no place she won't go. Mare and she brought a lot of their own baggage to the project. Jennifer played the older sister: wild, crazy, very loving. Just like my oldest daughter, Jennifer's sister in real life."

Turner said she is quite pleased with the setting of Seattle for *Georgia* after all. "The city [in a film] is always a character to me. It informs the work. And the Film Board in Seattle was fabulous. The music scene there is very strong too."

Not only did Turner get to be a producer on this film, but to work with one of her favorite directors, Ulu Grossbard. "He loves writers. And of course I was on the set. There is no hidebound rule to any of this: some directors let you on, some bar you. I think it's crazy to not have the writer there as a resource." In this context, Turner observes that a recent Writers Guild settlement is just one more step forward.

"Every time we go to the table and come up with some agreement, things just sort of move ahead, even if a little."

Many screenwriters have said that—unless a project is requested or backed by a star the stature of Julia Roberts, if not Roberts herself—it's very difficult to get a film made these days that is centered on a woman.

Nevertheless, Barbara Turner did write *The Company* (2003) for Neve Campbell, the Canadian native who once was in the National Ballet of Canada. "I researched the ballet in Chicago, though, spending time with the Joffrey Ballet there. Neve is a very interesting actress. And she misses working for the ballet. That's why I decided to write a film for her about dancing. I tried to make it an ensemble piece with the ballet company itself acting as sort of a character."

While some writers, like Nora Ephron, say they schedule a number of pages a day to write ("And if I finish by nine A.M. I go shopping for the rest of the day," says Ephron airily), Turner says, "once I get started I get compulsive and keep going and just kind of like to see where it goes." Also unlike most writers these days, Turner says she works in longhand because she feels closer to the work that way, and it seems more "organic" to her. Like many others, though, she says that she always starts her writing workday in the morning.

"Fitzgerald could write a mean [meaning terrific] woman," she answers in an initially negative answer to the question of whether a female is better equipped to write a woman's part. Thoughtfully, though, she adds that the "male writer's approach to writing women's characters may be different."

Turner says she has concluded that the best way to learn structure in writing for movies is simply to go to a lot of films. She says the same thing about dialogue. Her next big ambition—like so many female screenwriters and other moviemakers—is to direct. Surprisingly, given the topics she's previously picked, she says she wants to direct a thriller.

If Turner does not entirely recognize her work in the film *Pollock*, it might be because Susan Emswiller, currently a writer-director, also worked on the film. "The first time I met Barbara," she says, "was at a party after the film was finished." Emswiller, now a full-time writer-director, had some plays mounted at the MET Theater in Hollywood where she met Amy Madigan, Ed Harris's wife. "Amy liked three plays I had written based on the work of Edward Hopper, called *Brushstroke*. After she saw them, Ed Harris offered me the chance to work on *Pollock*."

Emswiller says that she was given the same biography to work from, and that perhaps it is inevitable that the two different writers may have chosen similar sequences. "I don't know that Ed was unhappy with Barbara's script; I do know that I was asked to write a script after she had finished hers." Emswiller goes on to say that you have to find the narrative in biography, which is not really a story. Her most recent film that she both directed and wrote is *In the Land of Milk and Money* (2004).

Working outside the Hollywood system, Emswiller—who started in the business as a set decorator—says that for her the whole reason to make a movie is to maintain her vision. "Otherwise it's just commerce."

Bending and twisting the cinematic form even more dramatically are filmmakers like Sally Potter and Lynn Hershman Leeson, along with other filmmakers mainly in the independent film industry, such as Patricia Rozema. Sometimes this is shown mainly in the form and format, as Rozema does in *Mansfield Park* (for graphic drawings and a lesbian kiss were no longer shocking in 1998), and sometimes in both form and subject matter, as in *I've Heard the Mermaids Singing*, with its unusual dreamlike sequences as well as its portrait of an accomplished professional gay woman and her lover.

It does seem, however, that filmmakers like Potter and Leeson change structure the most by deliberately picking material which will naturally alter the form of their movie. They even at times try to demonstrate that there may be an emerging connection among a female sensibility, certain "new" female-defined topics, and a less linear (read patriarchal) shape of a film, more free flowing in time and space. First person address to the camera and unexplained or unusual cutting are just some techniques used.

Sally Potter's *Orlando* shows this. Based on Virginia Woolf's stream-of-consciousness yet still chronological narrative about her love affair with Vita Sackville-West, a novel that spans four centuries and features a sex-changed persona, Potter cleverly uses first person to explain her protagonist's changes throughout the film.

The British writer-director who also did *The Tango Lesson* (in which she gave herself a role that came about because of her fascination with the tango) is from a bohemian English family. Born in 1949, she worked as a dancer and choreographer, and also managed to support herself as a filmmaker mainly (she has said in numerous interviews) by living cheaply, cutting corners on her films, even house "squatting."

Potter began making 8mm films as a teenager and later made several short films at the London Filmmakers Co-Op before training at the London School of Contemporary Dance and forming her own dance company in 1974. She returned to filmmaking in 1979 with her black and white short film, *Thriller*, which played at numerous festivals worldwide. Her feature film debut was in 1981 with *The Gold Diggers*, a story about the circulation of gold, women, and money. Subsequent projects have included the TV film *Tears, Laughter, Fear and Rage* in 1986, a four-part series on the politics of emotion.

While Potter's attraction to *The Tango Lesson* (1997) was straightforward—she liked the tango, she's always liked dance—the motivation for making *Orlando* was much more theoretical and complicated. Potter, who lives in England, discloses, "I found it a very liberating book because it broke all boundaries of time, gender, space, and place in a very light, kind of intoxicating way. It was as if Virginia Woolf was really in love with history and with imagery and, of course, in love with language. I remember the book burning its way visually into my mind."

One highly regarded study, *In a Different Voice* by Carol Gilligan (criticized at the time it was published in the 1970s in that it was considered retrograde), concluded that women do indeed think in less linear ways, and that this kind of tangential thinking is also used for relationship issues. Other psychologists call the female brain dendritic, or branchlike, in its thought processes. For backup, Gilligan quoted child psychologist Jean Piaget and feminist psychologist Jean Baker Miller, who asserted and "proved" (in the 1970s) that women indeed may think differently and that there is nothing is wrong with this. Some of her conclusions are that time is less linear for women, all levels being present at once. Curiously, or perhaps not, much of this is congruent with the simultaneity of time and place made possible by crosscutting, a characteristic of cinematic technique.

Recent research on brain differences between men and women have borne out Gilligan's thesis—it is now politically acceptable to explore those differences. It is even the basis for a recent book, the prize-winning *The Alphabet Versus the Goddess* by Leonard Shlain, which cites the Internet, movies, and television as partly responsible for the return of "the Goddess," or the feminine principle. Consequently, right brain activities are beginning to prevail again. These include nurturing, multitasking, empathizing with others, playfulness: a kind of laundry list of character-driven filmmaking. Men, according to Shlain, were single-minded hunters and gatherers, and the left side of their brain became more developed. Shlain uses Sandra F. Witelson's research in brain activity to support his thesis. Witelson found that women have from 10 to 33 percent more neuronal fibers in the front part of their brain, making them more sensitive to the moods of others and also more able to express emotion than men.

A "listening study" of twenty men and twenty women use the left side of the brain—traditionally associated with understanding language—to pick up conversations. But women also used the right side. Dr. Joseph T. Lurito, assistant radiology professor at Indiana University School of Medicine, said: "I don't want to provoke a battle of the sexes. I just want people to realize that men and women may process language differently." Presenting evidence at the Radiological Society of North America's annual meeting, he suggested women may need to use more of their brain to listen to conversations, with a positive side effect that they can listen to two conversations at once. The study used functional magnetic resonance imaging to support its research.

Simultaneity, usually by cross-cutting, is one of the aesthetic hallmarks of cinema that might make women comfortable with scriptwriting. And in the novel form, Virginia Woolf (along with James Joyce, of course) was the pioneer of this technique. So it is informative to look at a recent adaptation of a Woolf novel into film, *Orlando*. (Both in literature and in movies, audiences have grown adept at following a style which can jump around at will in time and space.) But when stream-of-consciousness was introduced to some perplexed readers in 1916 by James Joyce, one of the explanations for his technique was that it was cinematic. Virginia Woolf counted herself as one of his aficionados and followers, as shown in her homage in the beginning of *Mrs. Dalloway,* with its reference to Bloomsday on June 16, the day *Ulysses* took place.

In *Orlando*, the main part is taken by Tilda Swinton who plays all the roles in Woolf's parodic biography of a character who lives from 1500 to 1928 and who, inexplicably in the late seventeenth century at age 30, changes from a man into a woman. By topic then, and not just implication, the novel highlights questions of identity and the relation of sex, gender, and subjectivity.

In Potter's film, the voiced-over narrative of the film might have been expected, as there is a first person narrator in the novel. What Potter has added is moments when the main character turns to the camera, much in the manner of a stage soliloquy, pulling in the viewer with complicity. And while both the frame of the film and the direct address are contemporaneous with the viewer's experience of the film in the present, the voice-over is retrospective, speaking of past events.

Two critics writing about Potter in *Literature/Film Quarterly* have asserted that such "temporal disjunctions and narrative complications establish the radical difference between literary and film narratives, a significant difference that Potter works to her advantage to link narrative instability to the problematic construction of gender identity."[2]

The British feminist critic Annette Kuhn, taking a structuralist approach, observes that direct address and other techniques in *Orlando* "sever the twin purposes of anti-illusionism and self-consciousness in order to subvert conventional cinema." In her explication of the distinctions between conventional and alternative or counter cinema, Kuhn demonstrates how spectator/text relations are constructed and subsequently may be subverted within dominant film, challenging the order of things.

Orlando of course is not in mainstream, or dominant, film mode, so this kind of "against the text" analysis is not required. Instead, the very kernel of the novel and film is directly taken to the viewer. And Potter has used the multisensory quality of film to even further drive home Virginia Woolf's point about her hero/heroine: "Same person, different sexes."

One obvious change is that Orlando's heir in the movie is a female rather than a male, and a young girl is playing with a movie camera rather than a pen at the end of the film (an ending advanced a number of decades beyond the late 1920s when the novel ends). For Woolf, one of her points was that her lover, Sackville-West (a.k.a Orlando), was deprived of her estate because of her sex: the novel supplies a male heir in the end. But by making the male/writer into a female/filmmaker, toying with a camera at the end of the movie, Potter has given a different slant to the message, with a crystal clear commentary about motherhood and creative endeavors:

The ending I rewrote, and then rewrote again—yes, she will have a child, no, she won't have a child, yes, she will have a child, no, she won't. And I realized that it was a sort of symbolic dilemma within the story that echoed the dilemma that I'm sure many of us feel in our lives. The reason for keeping the child and for having Orlando be a mother is, first of all, because the majority of women experience motherhood at some point.

But I thought it was much more interesting for Orlando to have a daughter than a son because, within the story line, it would mean that Orlando would lose her property. I found that more interesting—the idea of Orlando finally, if you like, emerging from the shackles of the property-owning classes, emerging simply as a human being in her own right, not having to justify her existence through inheritance and not having the male line to carry on her name. Also because it's, in a way, time for women to take up our inheritance, an inheritance of a different sort. That's why the daughter is, at the end, playing with a little movie camera.

Perhaps the timing was uncannily right—the gender-bending idea, while still enough of a novelty to attract attention, had mainstream exposure by the early 1990s—but *Orlando* was a surprise for having achieved the commercial success it did. (It took Potter four years to raise the money to make the film.)

An even more conscious and purposeful manipulation of form was worked by Lynn Hershman Leeson in her 1998 movie *Conceiving Ada*, an imaginative and surreal look at the life of the daughter of Lord Byron, and once again starring Tilda Swinton. Ada was a mathematical genius and the inventor of the world's first computer language.

"When I first learned about Ada," says Hershman Leeson, "I couldn't believe I'd never heard of someone who changed the entire direction of the twentieth century. In fact, she was invisible historically and when I realized Ada had been just a footnote, I knew I had to give her a voice to speak to the current computer-obsessed generation." Like her father, Ada Lovelace was a free-spirited and fiercely curious woman. Ada had affairs with some of her generation's leading minds, including Charles Babbage, designer of the "Analytical

Engine," now regarded as an early prototype of the computer. She created a mathematical plan for the machine's calculations, and predicted that the machine could be used to produce images and sounds, thereby suggesting the world's first computer program a century before its time.

Conceiving Ada gives a picture of the world of computing as both sexy and feminine, and Ada as an adventurous romp. Providing a context to illustrate women's progress since Victorian times, Hershman Leeson parallels Ada's life with a contemporary plotline about a computer whiz who channels Ada via the Internet.

Hershman Leeson shot the flashback scenes in six days by digitally superimposing actors within virtual sets of Victorian interiors—a technique she invented, inspired by Ada. "I want people to know that history surfaces eventually, that what we contribute will have an effect, even if it's forgotten for a time," says the director. As well as being a filmmaker (she wrote and directed *Double Cross Click Click* in 1995 and *Teknolust* in 2002), and a San Francisco-based university professor, Hershman Leeson is known as a multimedia artist whose computer-based interactive installations have appeared in museums across Europe. For her, the Internet "can create a really liberalized community because it gets rid of sexism and people start to communicate just with the essence of who they are. The prejudices don't matter." This kind of pan-arts approach can be seen in all of Leeson's work: films, videos, and collages.

Like artist Cindy Sherman, Hershman Leeson toys with a constantly shifting persona in some of her art. One literal foray into identity shifts was to live a double life: she took on the identity of a temp worker, living an entirely separate life apart from her existence as a married professor (her real life). With a new social security number, a studio apartment, and a suddenly singles lifestyle, the artist Hershman Leeson ultimately presented this experiment as a kind of performance art, playing with persona much as she does as a screenwriter-director-artist.

She also uses identity shifts in her film *Teknolust* (2002), with Tilda Swinton playing a biogeneticist who uses her own DNA to create three "Self Replicating Automatons": Ruby, Marine, and Olive. All four roles are taken by Swinton. The film presents characters who seek love in a world where sexuality has becoming an outmoded means of reproduction. Contemporaneous with British dramatist Caryl Churchill's play *The Number*, with its more obvious references to cloning about which it cannot seem to make up its mind (three sons to one father: Sam Shepard in the early run of the show in New York, 2004–2005), *Teknolust* is more pro-emotion and pro-human connection.

Hershman Leeson is a tenured professor which gives her autonomy and some degree of freedom in her art; Potter is well known for both "getting by" and for getting grants, and lives in the more arts-friendly community of England. Yet Jane Campion, in the film-supportive countries of New Zealand and Australia, has been free to play with form and style even within the feature and mainstream film format. She has developed a different style for each of her movies, a style that is aesthetically concongruent with some of the new female emotions she's exploring. Audiences and critics alike, for instance, truly "turned on" to the dramatic editing and gothically, sometimes grotesquely beautiful and wild New Zealand scenery served as an emblem for female sexuality suddenly coming free in *The Piano*.

Holy Smoke (1999), though neither a critical nor commercial hit, also strove for a look which would reflect its heroine's emotional state. There are numerous swirly scenes that show the deliriously happy, highly subjective mindset of Kate Winslet's character in *Holy Smoke*, when she is initially submerged in cultdom in India, then the inverse as she is deprogrammed by Harvey Keitel and tricked home to Australia by her family. Filled as they are with flower child/flower power cartoon-like images, the blissful mental states of Winslet don't work very well. Perhaps that era is too recent, or perhaps Campion used clichéd images such as exploding lights and daisies swirling about.

More effective are the frightened and frightening moments when Winslet is being deprogrammed. These dark scenes on the isolated land where she is holed up with Harvey Keitel remind the viewer of the opening of *The Piano*: the frightening trip from England as experienced by Holly Hunter in that film, to be surpassed by the emblem of her identity, the piano—itself almost a person—bumping along the sea bottom at times, darkly and mysteriously finding its way (like its owner) to the distant New Zealand shore. Or the evocative scenes where she meets with her sharecropper lover Baines (Keitel), who has purposefully taken on the trappings of an indigenous Maori native.

Unusually creative in its mix of time, voice-over, and cinematography is the scene where "mute" Ada nearly commits suicide by tying her foot to her piano, which she instructs be tossed overboard as she is going away (this time with Baines) again on a voyage by sea. Being pulled down to death attached to her beloved piano among the fishes, Ada's voice-over narration suddenly announces to the audience, much in the intimate, if ironic fashion of *Orlando*: "Surprise, my will has decided to live." We then see her head breaking water, and she is pulled back into the boat.

These sequences are typical of what I would call Campion's signature visual style: intense, twisty, overwhelmingly subjective if finally liberated: always breaking out, or through. Perhaps they are examples of what British semiotic critic Laura Mulvey has highlighted in her influential essay, "Visual Pleasure and Narrative Cinema," in the well-regarded British journal *Screen* in autumn, 1975. Mulvey writes, "Quite apart from the extraneous similarities between the screen and the mirror (the framing of the human form in its surroundings for instance) the cinema has structures of fascination strong enough to allow temporary loss of ego while simultaneously reinforcing the ego."

All of the aforementioned films are special, made by special women, free for various reasons to work as they see fit: whether in Turner's case, because she has chosen progressive projects and people to work with; or in Campion's, because she is backed by a film community in her native country that supports experimentation and women's art; or in the case of Potter and Leeson, because they have broken away from the tradition of mainstream films. They have managed to move things their way, molding the shape of their films for their own reasons, and finding a format which expresses the point of view of their female heroes.

A larger challenge was faced by Callie Khouri, who was working as a producer of movie videos when she wrote down the idea for a script: "Screenplay idea: two women go on a crime spree. They're leaving town, both leaving behind their jobs and families. They kill a guy, rob a store, get hooked up with a young guy."

The movie became *Thelma and Louise*, an Oscar, Golden Globe, and Writers Guild Award winner for Khouri's script in 1991–1992, and the object of much attention-getting controversy at the time about the justifiable validity of women's rage. Reacting to the raised consciousness about women's roles, Khouri says she wrote the script as a kind of protest against Hollywood's tendency to limit women's roles to "bimbos, whores and nagging wives."

Khouri came to Los Angeles to study acting, working as a waitress and music producer to support herself. When *Thelma and Louise* became such a big success, Khouri says she was (and still is) baffled. "Men, women, everybody, they kept talking about the message of *Thelma and Louise* like it was an instructional video or something. If you're making a movie for women, you have to be very careful because they're not going to know the difference between fiction and a direction to take action. People would say, 'It's a very insulting depiction of men.' I'd be like, 'What's more insulting than *Natural Born Killers* or *Reservoir Dogs*? That's not an insulting depiction of men?' Why isn't anyone worried about those movies? It was all kind of jaw-dropping."

But Khouri also wanted to direct. In the end, it was nearly ten years until this came about, and in the genre—the woman's film—she both created and then resisted. The movie was *Divine Secrets of the Ya-Ya Sisterhood*. "I thought—the woman thing, I've done that . . . But then I thought, "Oh, shut up! There's nobody else doing it, you might as well." Once more as with *Little Women*, it took a handful of persistent females. "When *The First Wives Club* hit the $100 million mark in 1996, they said 'fluke.' It's a constant battle," said Bonnie Bruckheimer, a producer who fell in love with *The Divine Secrets of the Ya-Ya Sisterhood* even before it became a bestseller.

Bruckheimer says, "It had been around all the studios when it was in galley form and they all turned it down. And then they all turned it down all over again when I brought it to them. In the end Warner Bros. saw the light, thanks to a lot of wives and females on the staff. There was one young woman there who was relentless. I too was relentless since it was my last place to go."

One of the changes and challenges for Khouri was to make the older Ya-Yas, played by Dame Maggie Smith, Shirley Knight, and the Irish actress Fionnula Flanagan, the driving force of the plot instead of their more choric function in the novel, though some of the film's reviews commented that Khouri was unable to keep some of her superstars' performances under control. (The more standard Hollywood way of directing and filming *Ya-Ya* might have been to put the "pretty" heroine in front focus and keep her there, rather than stress the intergenerational themes, with emphasis on the older generation.) And in playing one of those older roles, Flanagan says she very much liked having the director and the writer be one and the same—it was easier to make script changes, as the daily demands of the set required.

The story still turns on Sidda (Sandra Bullock), a New York playwright who is feuding with her flamboyant mother Vivi (Ellen Burstyn). As they do in the novel, the mother and daughter have what seems like a final break, until Vivi's lifelong friends and member of her secret sorority (Knight, Smith, and Flanagan) come forward to broker a peace accord.

In the book, Sidda is placating and seems to be seeking her mother's love. Khouri has made Sidda a more independent and stubborn daughter who has to be kidnapped to go home to Louisiana, allowing for more narrative action.

While Khouri may have widely expanded the buddy genre for women, *Ya-Ya* is still within the tradition of the woman's film. (Studio heads Irving Thalberg and B. P. Schulberg needed and valued the "woman's touch" of women writers in defining many women stars of the 1930s and 1940s; even Jack Warner, who disliked women writers, felt he had to employ some to write for his major women stars in the era when women's films were an admitted, and clearly defined, segment of the audience.)

"These [including *Something to Talk About*] are emotional action movies, not physical action movies. There's no guns, no car going off a cliff. But there are emotional, inciting events and catastrophes," acknowledges Khouri. Whatever work Khouri will undertake in the future, it's clear that with *Thelma and Louise* and to a lesser extent in insisting on not reworking *Ya-Ya* to a glamorous Hollywood format, she carved out a permanent place for herself in the canon of women writers who have founded and worked a new cinematic paradigm.

And beyond that, *Thelma and Louise* was an appropriation of a formerly exclusive male form. Perhaps this is ultimately why the film was so disturbing. Some viewers and critics were stung by the vision of angry, vengeful, and violent women, and this is what the media concentrated on. Yet angry women bent on revenge, or even going against the law, have been on film before, whether or not the script was written by a women.

It must have been something else that made *Thelma and Louise* so revolutionary, and in this author's opinion it was that they took over the male, macho form of the buddy on the road movie. For complementary considerations of the use of the car in the film, see *High Contrast: Race and Gender in Contemporary Hollywood Film* by Sharon Willis. Willis asserts in her incisive chapter on *Thelma and Louise*. "Finally," says Willis, "this is a story about women and cars. What happens when women drive cars, instead of adorning men's cars, instead of sitting, fixed and still, draped across them? What happens when women wear cars instead of clothes? What happens when women strip down for a purpose that exceeds, bypasses, or falls short of sexual display."[3]

In my interpretation, the reverse gender remaking of *Butch Cassidy and the Sundance Kid* was the real provoking factor. For instance, there is even the scene of jumping into a river—the *Butch Cassidy* conclusion—transformed into Thelma and Louise's driving off a cliff at the end of the film. The movie's heroine may have taken a guy's life, but Khouri took a genre. In Hollywood, this may be been much more radical.

So . . . women screenwriters can successfully borrow or steal a male form. Or they can change a film's structure by letting it be dictated by unusual subject matter. True, this will not work for a big studio product, but this wasn't what they had in mind anyway. Turner may have had her script altered to suit Ed Harris's ultimate vision in *Pollock*, but it was her unique pitch which got her the gig. Both Sally Potter and Lynn Hershman Leeson have insisted on a highly individualistic format. They can afford to. They don't have big money corporate backers to report to.

Chapter Five

Adaptation

In thinking about adaptation, one of the easiest cinematic forms to spot, it seems the form that is most natural for women screenwriters to master is the novel. Especially if—as in the case of *Waiting to Exhale* or *Postcards from the Edge*—it's your own novel that is being adapted.

For one thing, the epistolary tradition on which the novel form is based seems the perfect format for female writers. In the tradition of Western literature, *Clarissa* and *Pamela* express a keen female sensibility that critics and historians of the novel have marveled for years at how closely author Samuel Richardson identified with his heroines and how completely and precisely he expressed their points of view.

Today, the author of what is acknowledged as the very first novel, *Tale of Genji*, is by general consensus agreed to have been Lady Murasaki Shikibu in the eleventh century. (Before this, the formal study of British literature categorized the novel as having grown from two strains, both starting in the eighteenth century. There was the realistic narrative, the chief example traditionally being Henry Fielding's *Tom Jones*, and there was the novel of sensibility from Richardson.)

But beyond this, the novel form may be peculiarly appropriate for both women writers and readers. For if one is physically trapped or enclosed as most women have historically been—whether in a drawing room writing as Jane Austen was or isolated on the moors as were the Brontes—it is the one form that is private and accessible enough that one can enter it imaginatively by simply writing a letter. Or writing a novel.

And in just as sedentary and private a way, one can enter it by reading. The present-day analogy is the Internet, statistically said to be used more by women than by men, at least as of this writing.

There is even a congruence between what Jane Austen described as typically ironic, and now famous, self-deprecation as working on a small square of ivory (compared to the geographical and temporal range of *War and Peace* or *Middlemarch*). It's the most ambitious novel written by a female—George Eliot—at that point[1] to the "little" film that chats about human relationships exclusively, rather than "great deeds." Interestingly, a few male directors like Kevin Smith (*Chasing Amy*) have also recently been drawn to the "little" film centering on relationships.

It is a whole different story for women dramatists, and for dramatists adapting their own plays to the screen. First off, there is a formidable political and financial structure to navigate in order to get a play produced. Yet there are a number of exemplary women dramatists who have managed this today: Wendy Wasserstein, Beth Henley, and Jay Presson Allen. And in the 1930s, Catherine Turney, Vilma Delmar, and Frances Goodrich mounted their plays on Broadway, as did Lillian Hellman in the 1940s and 1950s. Most playwrights-turned-screenwriters are on record praising dialogue writing as superior preparation for writing for the screen, especially if they do manage to adapt their own work.

One of the most outstanding recent examples of cinematic adaptation by a female writer—particularly in that she won an Oscar for her script—was the adaptation of Jane Austen's *Sense and Sensibility* in 1995 by actress Emma Thompson (not to slight other actresses-turned-scriptwriters such as Jane Anderson or Barbara Turner). Like many screenwriters adapting novels, Thompson used some verbatim passages that show a development of character, contain a visual element that can be easily transposed to the screen, or that keep up a narrative drive that moves the action forward. For instance, the scene where the two sisters, Elinor and Marianne (Thompson and Kate Winslet), encounter Willoughby, the suitor who has led Marianne on, is constructed very much as it is in the novel: "At last he turned round again, and regarded them both; she started up, and pronouncing his name in a tone of affection, held out her hand to him. He approached, and addressing himself rather to Elinor than Marianne, as if wishing to avoid her eye, and determined not to observe her attitude, inquired in a hurried manner after Mr. Dashwood, and asked how long they had been in town. Elinor was robbed of all presence of mind by such an address, and was unable to say a word. But the feelings of her sister were instantly expressed. Her face was crimsoned over, and she exclaimed in a voice of the greatest emotion, 'Good God! Willoughby, what is the meaning of this? Have you not received my letters? Will you not shake hands with me?' "[2]

It is tempting to say here that Jane Austen is intuitively cinematic in her "scene construction" or, in any case, her visual sense. For instance, another passage is perfectly realized in the film: Winslet's overeager reddening face, her painful withdrawal, the decibel of her voice expressing agitation.

Other bits are added, however, in Thompson's script for the film. If anything they show the sensibility of the industry insider that Thompson very much is, in that a broad emotional appeal is being reached for. In the novel, Marianne falls ill, as she does in the film, but it is not climactic or melodramatic. In the movie, however, there is a near deathbed scene—not in the novel—where Elinor keeps vigil and even prays to her sister not to die ("Dear, don't leave me") and then goes on to say how much she would dread to be alone as well of course how much she would miss her sister. The scene is candlelit, in the brownish and gloomy style of chiaroscuro, something very effective visually, but again not in the novel. Also, nowhere in the novel does the besmitten Colonel Brandon carry Marianne home or show his devotion by waiting in the wings to see if she will make it through the dark night.

The end of the movie is obviously and broadly appealing too, when a visual equivalent of money—truly golden confetti—swirls around Marianne and Colonel Brandon just after their marriage. Surely not subtle, or Austenlike, but just as surely a visual wrap-up and emblem of the merger of money and marriage. Whether it is to one's taste or not (or would have been to Jane Austen's, though Austen herself has an afterword of a sort in the book that mentions Marianne's marriage), it is clearly in the time honored tradition of a Hollywood happy ending.

This is how the offer of a scriptwriting gig came to Thompson. When the Los Angeles public television station aired a British television comedy series consisting of short skits written and devised by the actress, an executive putting together *Sense and Sensibility* was struck by the writing, particularly by those skits not set in the present. "The writing was funny and sweet and romantic and real," remembers the executive, producer Lindsay Doran, who asked Thompson to adapt *Sense and Sensibility* for the screen.

Though she had written skits, Thompson had never written a full-length screenplay and was excited about the idea of translating one of her favorite authors for the screen. She began by dramatizing every scene in the novel, which resulted in 300 handwritten pages: "But then I got braver and tackled the real problem of restructuring the story. I also bought a computer."

Thompson wrote a number of drafts over the next four years, working one-on-one with Doran. "The novel is so complex and there are so many stories in it that bashing out a structure was the biggest labor," Thompson notes. "I would write a version. Lindsay would read it and send me notes. Or, if we happened to be in the same city, we would sit down together and talk out the problems. Then I would cry for a while and then go back to work. And that's how it was for three years."

For additional insight into the story, Thompson plunged into Austen's personal letters. "The language of the letters is much less arcane than the language of the book; some of the sentences in the book go on forever," she says. "Austen's personal style was very clear and elegant. And very funny."

Of the final product, executive producer Sydney Pollack said, "She pulled off an extraordinary juggling act transforming a complex book into a strong story which never parts faith with the original. And her experience as an actress shows through in the way she instinctively knows when to let documentary truth give way to poetic reality."

Many actors, particularly highly intelligent ones, as the classically trained Thompson is, seem to want to at least try their hand at screenwriting, often directing as well. Creative control is always one reason actors give for this, yet in fact it is not such a new idea. Frances Goodrich, who started as an actress on the New York stage in the 1930s, became a playwright and ultimately a highly successful scriptwriter. Catherine Turney, the extraordinarily successful "woman's writer" of the

1940s (*Mildred Pierce*), started as an actress and playwright in New York City, always crediting her ability to write dialogue to the fact that she had worked as an actress. Though Goodrich, Turney, and Turner made the move to writing a permanent one, it would seem that Thompson and others such as Jennifer Jason Leigh will not jettison acting entirely, at least for now.

And though she now defines herself mainly as a writer, Carrie Fisher, the daughter of Debbie Reynolds and Eddie Fisher who played Princess Leia in *Star Wars*, says, "The acting experience has helped with the writing because you make dialogue that doesn't exactly work, work. Writing, you envision what would be easiest for you to say because you've been there." A novelist as well as screenwriter, Fisher makes her living by script doctoring these days. It is interesting to note that even though Fisher has four major scripts to her credit and has said she always wanted to be a writer rather than be known as the actress-daughter of Reynolds and Fisher, in fact she has over fifty credits as an actress, even if many are "just" cameos. She also has a cable talk show interviewing celebrities.

Fisher says, "In real life, people don't talk straight out in sentences, but in very particular ways." She also credits having performed as a chorus girl in some of her mother's shows: "The music gave me this particular sense of how sentences and scenes rhythm out and I feel that when I'm acting. When I write, I feel where the beats are, too, and I feel the acting as well. There's definitely a rhythm to the way I write."

Some, including Fisher herself, credit a diagnosed condition, like manic-depression, for their creativity. After working with Fisher, actor Meryl Streep said, "She has wonderful, undiluted inspirations. She has told me that she is sometimes reluctant to ameliorate a productive state by diluting it with medication."[3] Indeed, some of Fisher's connections are simply extraordinary, as is typical of a lot of writers, artists, and painters who get and keep creative by "yoking together by violence irreconcilable elements," as Dr. Johnson said of metaphysical poetry and John Donne in particular.

Fisher also has a very humorous, sideways take on things. For instance, the oft-quoted (if frequently uncredited) line in *Postcards* delivered by the then lesser-known Annette Bening, reassuring Meryl Streep about Bening's casual affair with the character played by

Dennis Quaid: "I'm just in it for the endolphins [*sic*]." Or the quirky bit at the end of the film when Shirley MacLaine's character asks for her eyebrows to be drawn on by "daughter" Streep before running the gauntlet of the press lying in wait for her hospital exit after a drinking-while-driving accident.

"Writing is something I would do anyway," says Fisher. "It's like homework. As a dropout, it's the best piece of karma in the world. You have homework for the rest of your life." She also told the *Hollywood Reporter* in 1989, "You don't necessarily have to be smart to be an actor, but you pretty much have to be smart to be a writer. *Postcards* gives me credibility, but it remains to be seen if I am a consistently good writer, or even, in some people's opinion, a good one at all. But the fact is that I do it, and in Hollywood, if you write, or have another talent besides being physically beautiful, people look at you differently."

In *Postcards from the Edge*, the dialogue is so cleverly observant of the push-pull of "relationships" that it seems only a female ear for dialogue could have come up with it. Like the writers of *Sex and the City*, Fisher exhibits the acute sensibility of someone who has been in the trenches, even obsessing about relationships, typical of mid-1990s female discussions.

When Streep's character, the Fisher stand-in, says to Dennis Quaid, "It's not that you sleep around. It's that you lie about it," Quaid replies, "That's what women always say. It *is* the fact that I leave. It *is* the fact that I sleep around." The same kind of acute mental recording about relationships and precise dialogue can be seen in Terry McMillan's *Waiting to Exhale*, the best-selling novel about four Phoenix, Arizona, African American women friends who bond and dish till resolution, if not retribution, about men takes place.

What has turned out to be a much-referenced set piece about female anger is in *Waiting to Exhale*: the burning down of the marital home by a furious wife after a spouse has gone. It is a scene with such an impact on the popular and "real" culture that Left Eye Lopez of the pop girl group TLC set her boyfriend's house on fire and was unabashed about it. She even claimed later it was cathartic and served as inspiration for the group's hit "Waterfall." A young girl in California who set her boyfriend's house on fire said she decided to imitate the behavior of Bernadine (Angela Bassett) in *Waiting to*

Exhale. Terry McMillan herself wrote the script for the film, directed by actor Forrest Whitaker.

There is a similar apocalyptic scene—featuring the revenge of the dumped wife—in the Faye Weldon novel *The Life and Loves of a She-Devil* and film *She-Devil*, which preceded *Waiting to Exhale* by six years. The renowned Susan Seidelman (*Desperately Seeking Susan*) directed the movie. Interestingly, both authors-turned-screenwriters McMillan and Weldon decided to keep their scenes of anger-exorcism.

She-Devil took some flack for being a bit grotesque in the way both Roseanne Barr and Meryl Streep were used and caricatured. (Streep, who played the wealthy novelist in the film, defended the movie by saying, "Those critics are mostly men.")

More successful was the use of the employment agency, Vesta Rose, that Barr's character starts up: a cinematic comic feminist set piece. To be able to pinpoint the most telling or emblematic section—such as focusing in on a female entrepreneur operating an employment agency for women, or to focus on the overdone plush pink interiors of the home of Streep's wealthy novelist (heart-shaped baths and all)—seems integral to what a successful adaptor does. (Along these lines Jay Presson Allen reminded me in the summer of 2001 that all of her movie scripts have actually been adaptations; when I told her that Robin Swicord's method for adapting was to jot down the themes she wished to emphasize, then mark out certain passages in the novel for an adaptation, Allen snorted, "Well, that's obvious, isn't it?")

Currently the most well-known adaptor for movies is Laura Jones, the winner of Australia's highest honor, the AFI Byron Kennedy Award. Jones did not start writing scripts until her late twenties. After six years of doing odd jobs ("I was never really trained for anything," she observes), she married and had a child.

"My daughter took up my time intensively for a few years. We were living in Canberra in the mid-'70s and the Australian film industry was just kicking off. I'd always loved film, but not television. I didn't grow up with TV in the house and didn't actually watch any until my mid-twenties. I saved up for a television set and after watching a number of drama programs, thought that writing them would be a way of making money without going out to work."

Jones sent a play to Tony Morphett, a successful screenwriter in Australia, and on the strength of it, he commissioned Jones to write for the Australian Broadcasting Corporation's series "Certain Women" in 1975. "You learn a great deal writing for soaps," she recalls fondly. "Too many people are snobbish about that sort of thing."

After working for television for a while, Jones wrote an original script, *High Tide*, a film about a woman (Judy Davis) who abandons her young daughter and then tries to reunite with her when she is an adult. Directed by Gillian Armstrong, the film garnered high praise. Shortly after, Jane Campion got in touch with Jones, hiring her as a screenwriter for the television miniseries and ultimately the film, *An Angel at My Table*, adapted from famed New Zealand writer Janet Frame's novel. Ever since, it's been one adaptation after another, including *The Well*, *Oscar and Lucinda*, *The Portrait of a Lady*, *Angela's Ashes*, and *The Shipping News*. "I loved doing *An Angel at My Table*, and each time I've been offered something I really wanted to do, it's been an adaptation."

Of her work, Frank McCourt, who won a Pulitzer Prize for *Angela's Ashes*, declared in a note to me, "First I was flattered they wanted to do it at all. Then I met Laura Jones in New York and felt I was in good hands. She [and Alan Parker, the film's director] said they wanted to be faithful to the book. They were. Perhaps too faithful? Laura Jones is one of the most sensitive people I've ever met and her work shows it."

Jones compares adaptation to smashing a pot and remaking it. "I am much more tender in the beginning. After that I like to put the pot away and let the pot's spirit stay with me." She says each novel has its own set of problems, and she searches for "an organizing principle or interpretative key" with each work. For instance, in *The Portrait of a Lady* (1996), the proposal to Isabel Archer (Nicole Kidman) by exceedingly rich and respected Lord Warburton (Richard E. Grant) takes place a quarter of the way into the novel. "I took the proposal and put it in the first scene of the screenplay and then collapsed everything after that," she explains. "Here is a girl being offered everything and she refuses it." From this key scene, Jones developed the pattern of light and dark she had found in Henry James. "The story goes from light to dark and then steps out to the edge again at the end," Jones says.

In *Oscar and Lucinda* (1997), however, Jones decided to keep the narrator of the novel in the film as an organizing principle. "That enabled me to travel through the twenty-five years the story takes to tell," Jones says. "He could choose whatever he liked to tell the story."

Unlike so many screenwriters interviewed for this book, Jones declares she has never been interested in directing, though she does allow that she is attracted to working with "like-minded" directors; people with whom she shares a passion. One, obviously, is writer-director Jane Campion, and another is director Gillian Armstrong. About working with Armstrong on *High Tide* (1987), Jones says, "I found sitting in rehearsals terrific. I loved it. I can't see how a film can be made without the writer going to rehearsals. The script kept on being worked on in minor ways until the shoot. Gill [Armstrong] and Sandra [Levy, the film's producer] regarded me as very much part of the process and when some minutes had to be cut out, I was asked about it—which writers often aren't."

Clearly, novels offer narrative drive, "sweep" being the word critics most often use. Think here of Fannie Flagg's *Fried Green Tomatoes*, a film adapted from her own novel. The movie perfectly shows the filmmakers' use of geographical place: a sense of place, of roots, the evocation for which Southern writers like Flagg are so well-known. Consider the scene, for instance, where Jessica Tandy and Kathy Bates together walk down a country road.

This may seem at first to have little necessarily to do with the woman's film, or a female sensibility, but in this case the walk, the road, is used for a female set piece: the heart-to-heart talk.

Fried Green Tomatoes, a sleeper hit when it came out in 1992, was adapted (with the help of screenwriter Carol Sobieski) by the novelist from her own book. Flagg said about the film's success, "Truthfully, I'm stunned at the success of the film. People in Hollywood initially said it was just too special, that your chances of a hit are very rare unless you had a 25-year-old sex symbol and gunshots and violence and everything else. We certainly didn't have that." The film was nominated by both the Academy Award Committee and the Writers Guild for best screenplay. Thus, 1992 turned out to be a good year for women writers: Callie Khouri won every award going for *Thelma and Louise*, including of course an Oscar; Meg Kasdan was nominated for an Oscar as well, for *Grand Canyon*.

Jessica Tandy played a spirited nursing home resident and Kathy Bates her overweight friend, burdened by a middle-age crisis. Together they remember the friendship and bond between two young women (Mary Stuart Masterson and Mary-Louise Parker) who ran a café fifty years earlier in Whistle Stop, Alabama. One of the women rescues the other from an abusive marriage, and there is also a progressive picture of relations between the races and an independent woman's entrepreneurial spirit.

In the early 1990s, producer Sherry Lansing optimistically analyzed the film's success for the *New York Times*:

There's a huge market for films that deal with women's issues. *Thelma and Louise* did. So did *Fatal Attraction*. These films appealed to—for want of a better word—an older women's audience. That is, women over the age of 25. I hate to think that's older, but that's the way it is. But that large group of women—women in their 40s and 50s, women who grew up seeing movies as kids, part of our way of life—that segment of the audience can make a hit movie. And that's what's happened to *Fried Green Tomatoes*.

It is not, however, exactly what happened to the genre of women's films, or to an industry awareness of the audience segment Lansing refers to. Nor does it describe the difficulty of getting the film made. According to Flagg, the film was in the works for four difficult years. One of the film's producers, Jon Avnet, says, "*Tomatoes* was an impossible film to get made, because on the surface, its appeal is largely female. There were no male stars per se."

Crimes of the Heart (1986), the film version of Beth Henley's play, takes up similar "female" issues though the bonding is based on blood, for the movie is about sisters. The themes are the female-centered ones, which are familiar to us by now but which in the mid-1980s were somewhat surprising and quite innovative, such as Diane Keaton's obsessing over her one shrunken ovary. The movie has an episodic quality, though the narrative story line is simple enough: what to do with the family estate when the sisters' father dies?

Beth Henley is primarily a playwright who has successfully adapted two of her plays for film—*Miss Firecracker* (from the play *Miss Firecracker Contest*) and *Crimes of the Heart*. *Crimes* won Henley a Pulitzer Prize in 1981 and her first appearance on Broadway. It was the first drama by a woman to receive the Pulitzer Prize since Ketti Frings's version of *Look Homeward Angel* in 1958. A screenplay seemed an inevitability, and it was, starring Jessica Lange, Diane Keaton, and Sissy Spacek. Nominated for an Oscar for her script, Henley went on to adapt *Miss Firecracker* in 1989. *Crimes* has all the elements of prime feminist drama, though Henley has been quoted many times as asking just indeed what is feminism and how does it apply to her. "I write what I feel," she says. "I don't really feel representative of my time, but I do feel representative of my heart. And that's where I try to write from."

Also, she says,

I cringe at the word feminist. I always look that up. Okay, you're for female rights—well, of course! But I don't favor women over men characters when I write them. I just try to look at people more than as just the sexes and hope that it'll be more a human point of view rather than having some sort of agenda to show that women are better, because I don't actually think they are. I think some women are better than some men. I know that sounds equivocating, but it's just true. And some men are better than some women. But to me it's not a question of better.

Still, *Crimes* has sisterhood as its central metaphor: literal sisterhood, centering on three Magrath sisters (was "Ma" purposeful here?), and taking place in that most traditionally female place: the kitchen, where conversations about men, fertility, money, and life are held. Standard stuff by now, but even more prescient is Babe's murder of her husband because, she says, she did not like his looks. Shades to come of the Dixie Chicks' "Fly" about 15 years later, where another Southern gentleman is done in (in "Goodbye Earl," though for far more serious accusations, including wife-beating).

Henley, a native of Jackson, Mississippi, studied drama and acting in college but found only closed doors as an actor in Los Angeles. After several unsuccessful years of acting, she moved to Louisville, Kentucky, to develop her plays. So here is another actor-turned-playwright-turned-screenwriter. And perhaps some embryonic movement to create a troupe: Holly Hunter appeared in the original *Crimes of the Heart* on Broadway, then later won raves as another fey Southern woman in the film *Miss Firecracker*.

Today's most prolific female writer closest identified with women's issues is Wendy Wasserstein, whose Pulitzer Prize–winning *The Heidi*

Chronicles moved with ease from stage to television movie. The play, probably more than any other cultural piece of work, raised the issue of accomodating the biological clock to career goals. And it has been an open season on this topic for writers ever since. She also wrote *An American Daughter* in 1997, a television movie with Christine Lahti. The film centers on a woman's rise to political power, the potential impact of her alleged past sexual improprieties on her constituency, and of course the difficulty of balancing the demands of work and family.

For some, Wasserstein is considered to be truly the "voice of her generation." She is also one of a handful of dramatists who manage to make a living from their writing; obviously she has been able to platform herself into other more lucrative areas, such as writing for television, though she makes no bones about her take on Hollywood. "I took a meeting out there," Wasserstein says, "and one of the very young executives said to me, 'Wendy, it just needs more conflict. That's what drama is all about, you know.' 'Oh,' I said to myself, 'I'll get right on it and let Robert Brustein [head of the Drama Department at Yale, where Wassertstein studied] know,' " she chortles.

In trying to assess the contribution and fittingness of the adaptation form for women screenwriters, the ultimate grid may be writer-director Amy Heckerling's *Clueless* (1995), which—though it was popular enough with those who doesn't necessarily read nineteenth-century novels—is said to have been most appreciated by those who consciously compared it to the novel from which it was adapted: Jane Austen's *Emma*.

Heckerling says she based her film on the novel; of course, there are an extraordinary number of retentions from the original text. Both heroines are comfortable, even spoiled, and each concerns herself with superficialities. Also, they each pick up and make over a protégée, almost like a toy.

This brings up the question: are themes like this that include a social, or material, world more appropriate to the novel, and the cinematic, form? For the drama can be just bare props or even nothing on a stage, leaving description or physical reality up to the audience's imagination, whereas the novel can easily accommodate the richness and details of the physical world.

In this case, the depiction of a material world is most definitely both the Los Angeles of Cher and the provincial world of Emma.

And women, traditionally anyway, have been trained in the minutiae of dress, the details of social behavior, the observation of class and caste. "Those are just the shoes I crave," says Cher Horowitz, speaking a line that may have just as readily been spoken by Emma.

Clueless seems to fall somewhere between adaptation and homage, at first glance, with references to the text too close to be ignored. And statistics have shown that repeat and the most enthusiastic viewers of *Clueless* are those who know Austen's *Emma*.

Of similarities between the two main characters, Emma Woodhouse is part of the rich, upscale society of a "large and populous village" in nineteenth-century England, while Cher Horowitz lives in rich, upscale Beverly Hills. In Highbury, the Woodhouses are "first in consequence there. All looked up to them." Cher and her father are also among the cultural elite; he is a litigator, a prestigious and lucrative occupation in one of the most affluent cities in the world. Cher is also one of the most popular girls at her school. The description of Emma that Austen gives is also a description of Cher. She is "handsome, clever, and rich, with a comfortable home and happy disposition." However, both Emma and Cher are not as perfect as they at first seem.

Because of their wealth, both Emma and Cher are spoiled, in control socially, and tend to think quite highly of themselves. Both have no mother figures in their lives and overindulgent fathers. Cher has everything a teenage girl could want: money, her own Jeep, a huge wardrobe, and more. She spends her time and a huge amount of money at the mall; because her father is so busy with his court cases, he has little time to spend with her to give her guidance and discipline.

An example of Cher's snobbishness can be seen in the scene where she and her friend Dionne are explaining to Tai, her pet project, how to become more popular. Cher observes that Tai has already started to elevate her social status "due to fact that you hang with Dionne and I." Cher may be taking pity on Tai, but she does so with an air of arrogance because she knows she is from a higher social class.

Similarly, Emma decides that Harriet's "soft blue eyes should not be wasted on the inferior society of Highbury and its connections," and that the friends Harriet has already made are "unworthy of her" and "causing her harm." Even though she has never met the Martin family, with whom Harriet had stayed, she condemns them as "coarse and unpolished, and very unfit to be the intimates of a girl who wanted only a little more knowledge to be quite perfect." Emma's arrogance causes her to assume that Harriet's acquaintances are not good enough for her, and that they are holding Harriet back from a better social life and status, even though Harriet is in the social class she should be in. So, Emma embarks on a mission to advance Harriet. She "would take notice of her; she would improve her; she would detach her from her bad acquaintance, and introduce her to good society; she would form her opinions and her manners." Harriet is not clever and desires only "to be guided by any one she looked up to." She is perfect material for Emma to mold.

In *Clueless*, Cher sets out to "improve" Tai, the new girl at school and the counterpart to Austen's Harriet. Tai is obviously of a lower class than Cher; her clothes lack style, her hair is stringy and dyed a hideous red color, she has a thick Bronx accent, and she likes to take drugs. Cher decides to give her a complete makeover: a new hairstyle, new makeup, a new wardrobe. She forces Tai to exercise in order to improve her physique, and wants her to read "one nonschool book a week" to improve her mind. When Cher's stepbrother-boyfriend Josh states his disbelief, she proudly replies, "What, that I'm devoting myself so generously to someone else?" and Josh answers, "No, that you found someone more clueless than you to worship you." Cher answers back that she is taking "that lost soul in there and making her well-dressed and popular. Her life will be better because of me." It's easy to see that, like Emma, Cher is not just helping Tai out of the goodness of her heart, but to feed her own ego and pride.

One obvious reason for the popularity of Austen adaptations—aside from the fact that they deal with female issues—is that her chief concerns are those of the observable, material world: manners as well as morals, estates as well as mental or emotional states. (Though one sly observer said that Austen films and novels are so popular now, particularly in women's studies courses, because young women feel that they may pick up some pointers on how to get a husband.) These concerns are more appropriate to formats suited to depicting the material world: novels and movies, those forms to which women have always been most drawn. It is while walking along Rodeo Drive in total misery, for instance, that Cher does some soul-searching. What really bothers her is that Josh is mad at her. She begins to remember the good times she had with him, and suddenly realizes she is in love with him. The point here is that it is on Rodeo Drive where Cher experiences her realization; something palpable and therefore not difficult to bring to physical life (particularly if you are filming in L.A.).

In contrast with novels and movies, in general drama or the stage uses the sparseness of symbolism. In fact, the chief challenge of stage-to-movie adaptation is to "open out" the original text, to make it more of the material world, more palpable. Sometimes this poses a problem, and sometimes the filmmakers' imaginations are sufficiently up to it. But in giving form to the material world, clearly novels have an edge and are an easier fit than stage dramas.

In an interview with the *New York Times* critic Frank Rich at Manhattan's 92nd St. in 2002, playwright Arthur Miller put it succinctly: "It's easier to make movies from novels than from plays, though you know you're going to lose control when you make movies."

Have women been historically just more used to losing control over their work? Or to put it in PC terms: are women necessarily more adaptable in the workplace? And, does being aware of the surface details of the material world—the minutiae of fashion, manners, social intercourse—make women more connected with the novel form?

Chapter Six

The Independents: Finding a Perch, Having Their Say

Many contemporary women screenwriters who have worked in the independent mode seem to have decided or recognized from the get-go that the mainstream writing format, or corporate world of filmmaking, might not be for them. Some, like Rose Troche (*Go Fish, Bedrooms and Hallways*) or Donna Deitch (*Desert Hearts*), realized that their subject matter—gay and lesbian–themed material—might dictate the indie option. Others, such as New York-based independent filmmaker Maggie Greenwald because of the kind of material she was attracted to, came to believe that there might not be a place for them in the corporate atmosphere of mainstream moviemaking and chose another path. For others, like Allison Anders, who sees herself as an outsider, the independent film also has been an inevitable if not always easy point of entry.

Greenwald, for instance, started out working as a union film editor in California in order to support herself while she was learning how to write scripts. One property she wanted to make into a movie was *The Kill-Off* by Jim Thompson; Greenwald did adapt and direct the novel into film in 1989. "I took some heat for doing that film," she says, "because of the violence, and because it was an action movie. However what attracted me to it was that it *was* very dark, very noirish." (In the heyday of feminism, for a new woman filmmaker to make her debut with a violent male novel must have seemed quite odd. By the same—if flipped over—token, Greenwald also laughs when asked how she has escaped the clichéd label of feminist filmmaker for her 1993 movie, *The Ballad of Little Jo*, and answers, "I haven't.")

As she speaks in her non-air-conditioned office on a very hot New York City summer day, Greenwald, in her late forties, is still in wunderkind garb: unironed man's shirt and "work" pants with a military look. Her office is decorated with photos and work mementoes, the most eye-catching of which is probably the very dark looking poster for *The Kill-Off*. If a movie poster can look menacing, it does.

A native New Yorker who returned "home" after her stint in California, Greenwald—despite some mainstream success and the positive reviews for her 2001 film *Songcatcher*—says that every day of writing, fund-raising, and ultimately shooting a film is a struggle. Rather than going to large studios for her projects, Greenwald uses smaller companies that give her more creative leeway, but still they must be approached. (*Songcatcher*, for instance, was backed by the Independent Film Project; *The Kill-Off* by Palace Pictures.)

Particularly difficult, she says, is the fund-raising, or backing-gathering part. "That never gets any easier. But I force myself to do it. After I write in the morning, I make phone calls in the afternoon. Whenever I start to feel lax about it, I think of what someone said to me the first time I was at Cannes, as a 31-year-old first-time writer-director. She told me, 'If you want to get all the things you want, you'll have to get out of the corner.' That was very good advice."

Greenwald lives in Brooklyn Heights now that she has a child, she says, and comes into her office in Manhattan's West 20s every day. She observes: "We are all so busy it's hard to keep in touch, but we all know each other, and how we are doing."

"We" refers to independent women filmmakers including Rose Troche and Allison Anders, writer-directors who are scattered across the country, or just plain wildly busy, like independent producer Christine Vachon, who is in New York. Greenwald speaks admiringly of Anders in particular, whose autobiographical film about gang rape, *Things Behind the Sun*, recently was released to wide and generally favorable press coverage. "She's a darling of the press," observes Greenwald.

With the exception of *The Kill-Off*, an action film, Greenwald's other films have had progressive subject matter, with strong female parts. Both *The Ballad of Little Jo* and *Songcatcher* were composites of historical female figures Greenwald had read about and wanted to immortalize on film.

Little Jo stars Suzy Amis as a nineteenth-century woman tossed out of her wealthy New England family for bearing an out of wedlock child; "Little" Jo disguises herself as a man and heads west to work. With a loose and episodic story line, the narrative around Jo has her/him encountering issues of work, racial prejudice, sexual experimentation, as well as gender bending.

Jo heads to the frontier to find that even there the only way she can survive is to disguise herself as a man (inflicting a disfiguring scar on her face) and keep to herself as much as possible. She ends up in Ruby City, a frontier town where gold grubbers, sheepherders, and cattlemen clash and struggle for profits from the land. The film has some affecting scenes showing Jo struggling alone with her sheep in the snow-swept winter plains; and one of the film's feminist messages is that the isolation of spending the winter with only animals provides the only real respite for Little Jo, appalled as she is by the violence and nastiness around her.

Songcatcher is partly based only on the story of an actual musicologist (Olive Dame Campbell), who scoured Appalachia in the early twentieth century for original Scotish-Irish ballads of that region (Greenwald's film is set in the turn of the century, and does not name Campbell).

Of her heroine, Greenwald says, "I always find the reality is wilder than nothing I could imagine. In a film like *Songcatcher*, which was intended to be a patchwork quilt of different women's lives in the mountains at that time, the heroine is a real type of woman. Certainly not all of the spinster schoolteachers at that time were gay, like the sister in the film, but I'm sure quite a few have been. Some of these women lived covert but very fulfilling lives. It's another aspect of me saying what women's lives have been really like."

Greenwald continues to work with nonmainstream material, for instance the Lifetime TV movie *What Makes a Family*, which was executive produced by Whoopi Goldberg. It was based on the true story of a Florida lesbian mother's fight to maintain custody of her child after the death of her partner. (In real life, the lesbian mother happily won her custody battle in 1989.) Recently Greenwald has been directing films for television, an activity that has become a kind of fallback position for numerous independent filmmakers. She directed *Get a Clue* in 2001 for Disney, and *Comfort and Joy* in 2003 for Lifetime.

Allison Anders and Rose Troche also have turned to television, particularly HBO and Showtime. Troche is originally from Chicago, and the lesbian-themed *Go Fish* was critically well-received in 1994 after it screened at Sundance, hailed by critic J. Hoberman in *Premiere* as "extremely well shot and imaginatively edited" and by Martha Baer in the *Voice* as interesting because it's "what a bunch of dykes do when no straight people are looking." *Hallways and Mirrors*, about gay men, came out in 1998, and *The Safety of Objects* gained praise in 2001, with Glenn Close playing a sort of matriarch in an upscale suburban setting. After this, Troche wanted to do a film called *Low Life in High Heels: The Holly Woodlawn Story*, but it wasn't greenlighted; she did get a go-ahead for a biopic on Dorothy Arzner, and a commitment from HBO to do a series of shorts set in the suburbs: *Women in Love*.

Allison Anders came on the scene in 1992 with *Gas Food Lodging*, which received a rave from Janet Maslin in the *New York Times* after it debuted at the Film Forum in Manhattan. Maslin enthused, "Imagine *The Last Picture Show* shot in color and shaped by a rueful feminine perspective, in a place where women are hopelessly anchored while the men drift through like tumbleweeds." *Grace of My Heart* followed, a film about the music business in New York in the 1960s and the Brill Building, *Sugar Town*, a *Nashville*-like movie about the movie business in L.A., and most recently the autobiographical *Things Behind the Sun*, a film about Anders's own experience of being gang-raped.

Anders shot *Things Behind the Sun* in seventeen days on digital. She proclaims digital—both for its cheapness and accessibility—as perfect for the independent filmmaker. "It's a tremendous thing for women and for non-white filmmakers," she says. "We were shut out pretty early on from a medium we created along with men. Women were there [in movies] from the very beginning, and so were blacks and Indians and Mexicans and everybody else. With the invention of the studio system, you can point to the people who got rid of us all. So I always feel like film was somebody else's and I was just getting to use it for awhile. Whereas with digital I feel like, 'I understand what we're doing.' "

Since that time a number of mainstream filmmakers have started using digital, even Jean-Luc Godard, most recently in his *Histoire du Cinema*. When Anders used it for *Things Behind the Sun*, it was innovative for a name filmmaker to use digital for a big project. Another innovative tactic of Anders was to premiere *Things Behind the Sun* on television. "I had a theatrical offer and a Showtime offer and ultimately I wanted to make sure that people would see the movie. I didn't trust the way the theatrical distribution is working now for independent filmmakers. Even if you get a critic behind it and the reviews are good, it can't keep a movie alive long enough for word-of-mouth to get around."

Up from trailer trash roots, a single mother with two kids, Anders nevertheless managed to start making movies in Los Angeles in the 1980s. She wrote German director Wim Wenders (*Paris, Texas*) a kind of fan letter, they started corresponding, and Wenders hired her for one of his films.

Anders is outspoken in her criticism of the industry, which probably helps her relations with the press. In an introduction to a book encouraging young girls to take up filmmaking, Anders says, "As females, we have almost no voice on the big screen. Often we find our lives, feelings, and experiences grossly underrepresented. . . . Maybe you have a really whacked-out group of friends you can shoot endless commentary on. Or maybe there's trauma in your past—film can help you deal with that, heal over it, and help others heal too. Or maybe you have a totally screwed up family and want to find the humor there—so make a dark comedy."[1]

As an independent Canadian filmmaker who made a film with a gay sub-topic before it was trendy, Patricia Rozema has continued within the independent mode, even working most recently with the top dog of independent movies, Miramax Films. Rozema's first big success was *I've Heard the Mermaids Singing* (1987), a reference to the timidity and sense of futility expressed in the T. S. Eliot poem. *Mermaids* is a movie so creative, so unusual in structure, that it won Rozema her wide acclaim and brought her subject matter—in part a lesbian-themed narrative—into mainstream media play. Her protagonist Polly is a whimsical if wacky "temp" who works at the art gallery of a gay woman art dealer—"The Curator," she reverently calls her. The movie includes some fanciful scenes of Polly's fantasy life, flying Superwomanlike above the cityscape, or wearing a huge garden party hat, chatting, even pontificating, as successfully as the Curator. *Mermaids* won numerous independent film awards; it will shortly be re-released by Miramax Films, and has been named as one of the best Canadian films of all time, a surprising achievement for a movie, which comments about creativity and dilettantism, with its pioneering and matter-of-fact attitude toward being gay.

"I was not so much interested in the Curator's being gay, or Polly's devotion to her. What I wanted was to show Polly's interior fantasy life, and for this I had to create a totally new structure. Perhaps something one can only do in the independent film," says Rozema. The movie shows Polly's (the protagonist) dream state, her fantasy life, voice-over monologues to the audience, and even the intermix of cinema verité and traditional narrative forms. Of course men have fantasy lives too, but it is perhaps a uniquely female point of view that takes a secretary as a protagonist and examines her ambition, though she may not be particularly talented, or even bright. *The Dresser*, by contrast, is another film, though from a play, about a master-slave relationship, but it shows Tom Courtenay's wasp-like wit as occasionally balancing out his relationship with the overbearing actor played by Albert Finney. *Mermaids*, instead, takes up a perhaps more exclusively female concern—the often unquestioning devotion of female secretaries.

Rozema's innovative use of form is also seen in her 1999 interpretation of *Mansfield Park*, perhaps the most unusual Jane Austen novel adaptation to date. Rozema mined Austen's letters (as did Emma Thompson for her *Sense and Sensibility*) to expand the text and include more references to the real-life nineteenth-century slave estates in the West Indies, one of which is owned by the wealthy relative who takes in his distant poorer cousin, Fanny Price, played by then newcomer Frances O'Connor, an Australian actress. The estate owner in the film is a role brilliantly taken by playwright Harold Pinter; and at one point in the movie Rozema includes the quite shocking drawings in a notebook of some graphic sketches of inter-racial couplings of landowners with slaves. The social commentary here is critical of racism, sexism, and, of course, a caste system. The notebooks were not in the original Austen novel, nor are there any references to them in Austen's letters either.

Rozema says, "I don't want to criticize *Sense and Sensibility* [the film directed by Emma Thompson] because it had something good about it. It's my favorite recent Austen adaptation. I didn't much care for *Emma* at all. But *Mansfield Park* didn't lend itself to that kind of 'syrup on your candy' type of treatment; so I set out to make something that had an aesthetic that would appeal to me. I normally don't like costume dramas as they call them so I wrote it first as a contemporary drama and then translated it into the period. So I went from old to new to old again, concentrating on the kind of emotions or dynamics that are eternal, or at least last a century or two."

Rozema spoke about playing with form, and the mix of fiction with more fiction, what the writer-director herself calls metafiction. There is no question that this may be easier for the writer-director working in the more freely structured independent mode. Speaking about the main character of *Mansfield Park*, who retains some of the irritating characteristics Austen originally invested her with, Rozema said, "I couldn't figure out why Austen would write an annoying character; just one reason I was drawn to reading about her. I read a few biographies and I found this almost anarchic spirit in her when she was writing her first works especially; and I just thought it would be interesting to write this metafictional mix or something. It felt like a contemporary strategy to include the reality of the author and her other fiction into the script for *Mansfield Park*."

Rozema also added a lesbian layer: a kiss and numerous eye exchanges between Frances O'Connor and Embeth Davidtz's characters. Yet while this is an obvious Rozema addition to the film, she is most definitely not doctrinaire. "No," she says to the standard question about whether or not men and women write differently. "I think great male directors and writers can do good female characters and I hope I can write and direct good male characters. It's just silly to think otherwise."

Yet she admits that she has the freedom to work only on projects that interest her, as she does not need to be near to, nor dependent on, the moviemaking machine of Hollywood (or New York for that matter). "I'm not high maintenance," laughs Rozema, who still lives in her native Canada, outside of Toronto. "So I can afford to take a lot of time off in between films, to pick and choose what and when I want to work."

Rozema, born in 1955, lives in a semirural setting and has one child. She said she maintains an active interaction with a number of Canadian filmmakers, and praises the Canadian film industry in general for treating women writers and directors better than they are treated in the United States.

I think it has something to do with the fact that we're not a world power. We don't have the biggest dick in the world. It's not part of our identity to be the dominators so we have a tradition of women writers, strong women writers. Film, too, has been respected as more of an art form and more than a business. In the U.S. it's more of a business.

Women are allowed to be artists in Canada. I would make the same observation about Australia. There are more women writer-directors coming out of Australia per capita and in Canada than in the U.S. Not that there are a ton of women directors in Canada. It's a hard job and when most people figure out what it takes, they don't want it.

Echoing what Jay Presson Allen has said about the overwhelming totality of a two-year commitment if one wishes to direct a film, Rozema observes,

The hours and constant struggle of being a director are demanding, which is why I don't do it very often. I love having the writing stints in between. Writing makes me feel like a real human being. I get to actually really focus on something and I'm not out there promoting or organizing the world. So it's a nice rhythm. Interior for the writing and then exterior for the directing, then interior again for the editing and exterior again for the promoting and releasing of the film.

At the moment I can't wait to get back to the writing. Because it's all there. That's where movies are made. Movies are written. Actors flock to well-written things. The scenes direct themselves if they are written properly. It's really easy to know what the right thing is. When the scene is not clear, you don't know what the intention is: then you don't know where to put the camera.

In explaining her methods for *Mansfield Park*, Rozema asserts, "The main character is not fully drawn. What we do get from her is that she is sort of quivering and shy. There is so much else that is interesting about that novel. It's very different from the rest of Austen's work in that it has darker currents running through—the slavery business of course and even the whole atmosphere of sexuality in *Mansfield Park*. Plus, the authorities are not necessarily benevolent in the novel, and the presentation of poverty is much more extreme, a whole segment of the novel set in abject poverty." In *Mansfield Park*, Rozema used a technique she also cleverly employed in *I've Heard the Mermaids Singing*: the sudden monologue, or first person address, of the main character to the camera, or the audience, in a one-on-one confidential manner.

Polly is used in this framing device all throughout *Mermaids*, until the very witty conclusion with an even more interesting twist when she tongue-in-cheekily shows her boss/the Curator more of the realistic art that is similar to her photographs (work of Polly's that the Curator has made fun of) as Polly opens a literal "door" at the film's conclusion—with credits spilling over the screen—onto a scene of a real-life forest.

"Here," she says with a knowing wink to the camera, "Let me show you more." That is, a real forest, a real scene, so very far removed from the experimental and often ridiculous art shown in the Curator's gallery. There is a clever satirical swipe here at a gallery scene that eulogizes abstract expressionism with overblown critical talk at the expense of representational art. *I've Heard the Mermaids Singing* was made in the 1980s at a time when "the emperor's new clothes" spin on art was common.

The first person address is used more sparingly in *Mansfield Park*: Fanny is shown writing in her diaries, then turning to the camera and addressing the viewer. This kind of cinematic monologue seems to be a favorite hallmark of Rozema's and other independent filmmakers working today. One thinks of Sally Potter's use of this technique in *Orlando*, when Tilda Swinton turns to the camera to give her character's private thoughts, perhaps a natural for cinema verité-influenced independent movies too, when the presence of the audience is acknowledged.

Filmmakers such as Anders, Greenwald, Troche, and Rozema, now in their forties and fifties, seem to have needed or been forced into the independent mode to get their films made, their voices heard. At one point this was associated with a kind of purity in moviemaking; think of movies like those of experimental filmmaker Maya Deren.

Yet, ironically, contemporary independent women filmmakers have cleared a path for an entirely different kind of writer-director, those who start in the independent mode almost as a career choice with a structure nearly as set and predictable in its own way as an MBA or law degree. Stacy Cochran, Kim Peirce, and Patty Jenkins are typical of this new breed. Sometimes the "right" school seems to fit in with this plan too. In California it seems to be USC; in Manhattan it's NYU. In that one way alone, independent filmmaker Stacy Cochran broke form, going to Columbia Film School, a maverick choice but one that worked for her.

Though her most recent film, *Drop Back Ten*, did not receive good reviews, and subsequent projects have had trouble getting off the ground ("I'm not sure anymore how to get a movie made," she confided to me in the spring 2000), for a while it seemed that Stacy Cochran was a sure shot for a successful trodding of the indie path on her way to a wider success.

Cochran, from Passaic, New Jersey, hit it big in 1992 shortly after she graduated from Columbia Film School with the breakthrough success of *My New Gun*, a comedy about a bored New Jersey housewife played by Diane Lane. Cochran snagged the up-and-coming (at the time) distributor IRS Media, I profiled her for the *New York Times* shortly before the release of the film, and the movie was well-reviewed, even by the prestigious *New Yorker* magazine. Married to an attorney, living downtown in the heart of the burgeoning film scene, Cochran seemed unstoppable.

It is especially notable that within a year of graduating from Columbia, she made *My New Gun*, her first feature. At Cannes she was one of three American directors featured in the Directors Fortnight. A graduate of Williams College with a major in political science, though she says she always intended to write fiction, Cochran was working at a magazine in New York City when she decided to become a filmmaker. Experimenting with various literary forms, she started writing film scripts: "It was a better, bigger way of writing fiction. You could start with the language and not stop until every element was under control. But it soon became clear I was going to have to do it full time." She made a couple of small films on her own, and then decided to go to Columbia University's Film School. "The attitude at Columbia is: writing first. Don't get hung up on equipment. I learned to see directing as an extension of fiction, not an exercise in technology."

Of her work, the playwright Romulus Linney, who taught screenwriting to Cochran at Columbia, says, "In the beginning, her work did not show enough progression of a dramatic action. But she faced the structural problems and worked very hard on her writing. It's not that hard to make connections in the business. The hard part is the writing," concludes Linney.

Cochran says, "I felt like I had found my form. It could be a fluid change, too. And more interior." But once she starts directing, she says, the script is hard to improvise from; and most of her films are verbatim from the script. Cochran says she's instinctively a planner, but with a small budget film it's imperative to be ready for the day before filming starts, and deviations (or improvisations) can be costly. She describes a typical day of directing as getting up early, which most filmmakers know about. But she also adds that the night before, she must make extensive preparations so that not a moment or a budgetary expenditure is wasted. In such a case, it's easiest to stick to a script.

Most of Cochran's films are set in the suburbs. One short, *Another Damaging Day*, shown in 1990 at the New York Film Festival, is about a teenager who is struck by lightning while washing his car in the driveway. The tall, slender, henna-haired Cochran says she realizes that comparisons with Hal Harley, the well-known Long Island filmmaker (*Simple Men*, *The Unbelievable Truth*, *Trust*), who also focuses on suburban middle-class life, are inevitable. She is careful to point out that she has never met Hartley, and says, "I don't want to make the suburbs a dartboard. I don't believe that just because somebody lives in a house at the end of a driveway, they're less profound."

My New Gun, which came out in 1992 when Cochran was 33, was shot in less than a month in Teaneck, New Jersey. Then she shopped it around to film festivals in Toronto, Seattle, Boston, Chicago, and Cannes, and was the only woman selected for the prestigious Directors Fortnight of some twenty directors. She says she is always happy to introduce it with the following tagline, which she still feels describes the film: "The movie is about guns and women, but it's also about men and women."

Cochran wrote and directed *Drop Back Ten* in 2000, a film that featured James Le Gros, the actor she used in *My New Gun*. When it premiered at Sundance, *Drop Back Ten* was described by *Variety*'s reviewer as a "shaggy-dog comedy-drama so low-keyed it hardly registered." *Drop Back Ten* centers on an out-of-work journalist (Le Gros) with two ex-spouses who is writing an article about a film within a film, a football movie. Still working within the mode of social comedy, and firmly within the independent tradition, Cochran produced the film herself, as well as wrote and directed it. She still believes that writing is the cornerstone of her work: "I creep up on a story, get dreamy. It's like I'm walking through traffic with my nose in a book."

Another graduate of Columbia University's Film School, Kim Peirce chose that school for very much the same reason: its emphasis on screenwriting: "At Columbia you work with actors and write scripts, and the emphasis is more on story and character and less on production values. I was twenty-two at the time I went to Columbia. I think that writing is crucial to the process of directing. You can't make a great movie if you don't have a great character and a great structure in place. It all goes back to Aristotle, dramatic structure, three acts, etcetera. There is a certain momentum you need for a film and the more you study screenwriting, the more you will see that."

The child of teenage parents, Peirce is from Pennsylvania and was born in 1967. She went to the University of Chicago, but had to drop out after a year because of financial difficulties. Peirce lived and worked in Japan for a time before returning to Chicago to finish her degree. While in Japan she found she enjoyed photography, and when she came back to the United States, she studied photography; but after taking a film class, she changed gears.

At Columbia, Peirce wrote a script about an African American woman who had to dress as a white man in order to work as a spy during the Civil War. "Then in 1994, I read an article in the *Village Voice* about Brandon Teena, who passed herself off as a boy and seduced many different girls. When a group of kids discovered her secret, she was raped and killed for it. I realized that on a narrative level Brandon's story was exactly the answer to what wasn't working with my other film. I became obsessed with the story and went to Nebraska with fifteen transsexuals to attend the murder trial, and immersed myself in Brandon's tale."

To support herself, Peirce worked by night at a law office, where—with the full knowledge and even interested approval of the firm—she had access to computers as well as the more than 10,000 pages of court transcripts, including interviews with those involved with Brandon's case. She then took the project to the Writing Lab at Sundance.

But it wasn't until fellow filmmaker and friend Rose Troche introduced Peirce to producer Christine Vachon that things really started to cook. Even so, from start to finish it took more than seven years for the project to come together. Peirce says there were many times she thought the film was dead in the water, but was dramatically rescued by the Independent Film Channel, which gave her $1 million. Ultimately the movie was distributed by Fox Searchlight.

Boys Don't Cry is a very pure example of a female-created film in that Peirce wrote and directed it, there was a female producer, and both were actively involved with casting the movie.

Finding a girl who could pass as Brandon on film was key, and when we found her it was an event. We needed someone who had the charm and charisma not only to pass as a boy, but to gain entrance into people's lives. I was getting tapes from people all over the country who were transgendered and transsexual that could pass as boys, but couldn't act in the way that I needed. Because in 1996 it was considered taboo. But by 1998 the cultural tide had turned and it was now cool to be queer.

Hilary Swank sent a tape to Christine's office, and when she came to California for the audition, she passed as a boy to the office guard. I thought we had found our girl, and I hired her and took her to get her hair cut. And then we had this gorgeous teen icon before us who was a cross between Matt Damon and Leonardo DiCaprio.

One trend in the independent movie scene is that it has had successes in the past decade with lesbian topics: one of the "new" women's issues being openly treated by women writers. Among the underlying reasons might be that the gay community is very supportive of its members, providing a kind of instant networking. Or it might be just an idea whose time has come, culminating not only in the success of *Monster*, the independent film about the love affair between serial killer Aileen Wuornos and her girlfriend, but also the acclaimed Showtime series "The L Word," dealing with the lesbian lifestyle and subculture in America.

Boys Don't Cry showed on the festival circuit: the Venice, Toronto, and New York Film Festivals. Peirce credits early support from critics Roger Ebert and David Denby, who acknowledged Hilary Swank's performance, adding that the Oscar buzz for Swank came after the New York Film Festival.

Peirce's advice to aspiring writers and filmmakers is relatively simple: find out what turns you on about movies, and then learn everything you can about acting, writing, and dramatic conflict. But mainly be passionate about your subject.

Another success story is that of Patty Jenkins whose movie, *Monster*, won a Golden Globe and then an Oscar for Charlize Theron in the Best Actress category in 2004. What made the movie even more of a long shot is the fact that there had already been a recent documentary about Wuornos, and before that a 1992 made-for-TV movie with Jean Smart (both written and directed by men). Jenkins's script for the story is a slightly more fictionalized account, though still based on Wuornos's life, love affair, and her murders of the "johns" she took money from as a prostitute.

Patty Jenkins defines herself as a New Yorker, though as an "Army brat" she moved all over the world. Interested in the arts, she wasn't entirely sure in which direction to go. "I couldn't afford to go to college and then I heard about Cooper Union, which was free if you got in," she says. While there she studied painting but, like Peirce, changed career goals after taking an experimental film class. After graduating, Jenkins went to California and became a camera operator (perhaps even more difficult for a woman than to become a screenwriter). Working on commercials, music videos, and movies—sometimes for directors as well-known as Jonathan Demme—she also applied to and got into the American Film Institute Directors Program. Jenkins's thesis film was an official selection of the AFI Festival, and in 2004 she was given the annual award for director from the AFI program by Jean Furstenberg.

So here is one incredibly successful example of the film "career plan" of going to California, attending professional school there, and getting your foot in the door in the business. And not forgetting to make contacts along the way.

The idea for *Monster* was very much a personal inspiration, and had been on Jenkins's agenda for some time:

I wasn't a filmmaker yet when I first became aware of the Aileen Wuornos case, seeing her trial on television, but I became one later on. I wasn't thinking about doing her film but I have found notes from five years ago where I wrote the line "A *Raging Bull* style film about Aileen Wuornos." It had crossed my mind but I was planning on doing other things first, though I was surprised that no one had done her story really well. The opportunity came all at once when I mentioned to my producing partner, Brad Wyman, that I had always wanted to do that story and he said to go ahead because it would be relatively easy to get funding for a serial killer movie. The next thing I knew I was doing it.

She emphasizes, though, that after meeting and talking with Wuornos, she decided not to work with any folks who might cheapen the story. "As soon as I decided that I was going to do the film, I wrote to her. She wrote me back and we started a regular correspondence. Then suddenly the execution was scheduled and I wrote her a final letter. The night before she was executed, Aileen took a chance and decided to open up an archive of letters including some between her and her girlfriend. Oddly, I don't think Aileen would have revealed herself in person the way she did in those letters."

Writer-director Jenkins was surprised that a number of actresses were interested in playing the serial killer: "Wuornos was so hideously ugly I thought people wouldn't want to play her. I was shocked. A lot of them told me that actresses are looking for three-dimensional roles. That was a total education to me." Jenkins had seen Theron in *The Devil's Advocate* and subsequently screened all her other movies going back to 1995, admiring her level of commitment to each role. She says that once Theron was cast, the level of the entire film was raised.

Monster was shot in twenty-nine days, using many actual locations—bars and roadside pit spots—in a ragtag section of Central Florida. According to Jenkins, "*Monster* is a performance film. Whatever accolades there are, I knew it was a character move and the best thing to do was to get a great performance." Though the scenes of violence were initially difficult to shoot, Jenkins says once she got into it and reminded herself that it was all based on reality, she had no problem with writing or directing violence.

Monster, intriguingly, answers a number of questions about the new female-written "woman's film." It definitely is a character-driven movie, yet there are scenes of intense and unexpected violence. Additionally, at times it functions like an action film, with roadside scenes of rage and revenge. It even has a protagonist we like in spite of the fact that she is violent, and sometimes mean. And because she is so in love with her girlfriend, played by Christina Ricci, we even accept some of the horrific things she does: turning tricks, taking money from and then murdering her "johns."

So, a woman writer (here Patty Jenkins) can write and handle violence, and even transform a character-driven movie with all its emphasis on emotion into that mainly male bastion: the buddy "on the road" movie. *Monster* gives a resounding "yes" to every "can they?" question posed about the abilities and proclivities of women screenwriters.

Chapter Seven

The Pragmatists: Moving between Film and Television

While in the current era of market-driven filmmaking, many women screenwriters have deliberately or by default chosen cable television or the independent scene, a few female writers (and writer-directors) have still managed to happily and readily move in and out of various genres and media. Jane Anderson is one, a former actress who has successfully written for television and for features. She intends, it would seem, to keep moving back and forth as the material dictates, and as it pleases her.

A cheerful woman in her late forties, Anderson is now trying her hand at directing, though she does put a limit on this activity. "When you direct, it's almost like a year out of your life, and you may have to be away from home. I'm very wary of that now, as I have a small son. My partner is the full-time mom, but I don't want to be away from home for that long either." Anderson declares in a very matter of fact way, "I'm gay."

She also adds, "Now that I'm a director, I understand directorial problems much better than when I was a resentful screenwriter."

Originally from Northern California, Anderson now lives in Santa Monica, apparently the region of choice for many screenwriters. According to her, it's necessary to be in L.A. for at least the beginning of a screenwriting career, but ultimately these days it doesn't much matter where you are. Anderson adds, "Starting out, you must depend on the generosity of people in positions of power."

For Anderson, one of those people has been Jodie Foster, with whom she made a connection after the huge success of Anderson's for television movie, *The Positively True Adventures of the Alleged Texas Cheerleader–Murdering Mom*. Under Foster's aegis, Anderson wrote and directed the feature *The Baby Dance* starring Stockard Channing and Laura Dern. Though *The Baby Dance* made its first national appearance via the indie film scene, including the Independent Film Market venue in Manhattan, it's a guess that the imprimatur of Egg, the Foster production company, brought more recognition than most independent films might otherwise receive.

Following her modus operandi for *The Texas Cheerleader–Murdering Mom* gives some indication of how Anderson works. The movie for television was based on the real-life murder of a cheerleader by the mother of another would-be cheerleader, who had lost the contest to be on the cheerleading team. As bizarre as this sounds, Anderson says that her understanding of this incident became more lucid after she visited the tiny Texas town where the incident took place:

I researched for two or three days in Channelview, Texas, which is plenty of time for such a thing. When I was in Channelview, which is a kind of dumping ground for the oil fields (the economic basis of the area), I saw that the people had little to live for except cheerleading and football.

These people were living in a kind of toxic dump or wasteland. The environment was filled with toxins from a petrochemical plant, plus there was the ubiquity of shot guns. And when the plant blows up in the movie I feel it was a metaphor for Wanda's turning point: an externalization. [Wanda, played by Holly Hunter, is the mom of the movie and incident.] At that point she decides to get a hit man.

Anderson says she believes that "as writers, we should let the research inform what conclusions we draw, not the other way around. That is why I always tell people that when I am assigned something, I insist on going to the place of the film. I really feel I'm a cipher for the material."

Though *The Texas Cheerleader–Murdering Mom* may have been a turning point for Anderson in that after its airing Jodie Foster called her "into the office," Anderson's involvement with the entertainment business is not new. After college, she went to New York to try to make it as an actress. This led to a seven-year stint as a stand-up comedian. Anderson says she honed her craft in a group in the 1970s, which included Anne Meara and Jerry Stiller; the group was called The Writer's Craft. Billy Crystal spotted her at the Duplex, and asked her to come to California to work on a TV show.

With the attitude of "that's the way it goes," Anderson says the show only lasted one week. Wanting steadier work, she wrote a spec script for television, and got her first job as a writer in Los Angeles: for the television show *The Facts of Life*. "Working on this series taught me to not be precious about my words. I learned how to detach from what I was doing."

Anderson says sometimes she will get an idea for a movie and pitch it, and sometimes just get an assignment. For instance, the day I interviewed Anderson, she was trying to find out more details about a news bit that intrigued her, though it was proving elusive. Somewhere she says she heard about an American woman reporter captured by the Taliban, and thrown in jail. But the woman was so obstreperous and very much an obnoxious demanding journalist—wanting a better room, food, telephone privileges, and the like—that ultimately the Taliban released her. Anderson felt that this would be the kernel for a great movie for television, and whether or not she ever finds out more about this tidbit and gets the film made, you have to agree that such a movie would be quite funny and of course timely.

"I write whatever intrigues me and then offer that. But in the case of *When Billie Beat Bobby* [the made-for TV movie about the 1973 Billie Jean King and Bobby Riggs match], that came to me through ABC.

"One thing I'm not interested in and never have been is thrillers or violence. I don't do a film unless I feel it will enlighten people in some way."

A feature which earned a great deal of acclaim for Anderson in 1995 was *How to Make an American Quilt*, an ensemble piece with what seems today to be a quaintly feminist theme of generational wisdom being passed down via the communal work of quilt making. Contrary to the cynicism expressed by a number of contemporary women screenwriters, Anderson observes, "I don't believe it's not possible to get something like *How to Make an American Quilt* made these days. Quality things always get through somehow. Just check out the nominees every year at the Oscars. There's always at least one wonderful thing. It's not easy, but they do get made."

Anderson says she loves the freedom of writing for cable and Home Box Office, and suggests that this is an especially good way for a writer to get a foot in the door. Her advice to up-and-coming screenwriters urges that they "write from the heart. Write about what you love and not what you think people might like. Of course, be open to rewriting." She also says that, unlike a lot of screenwriters of both sexes these days, she never writes a potential project with a star in mind.

Also unusual is that Anderson says she never encountered prejudice because of being a woman.

Yet perhaps the most distinctive thing about Anderson is that she sees herself as free enough to move at will from one form to another. For instance, she adapted her own award-winning play for television: *Normal* (2003) starred Jessica Lange and Tom Wilkinson as a happily married couple until he decides he wants a sex change operation. "I don't consider myself tied down by a genre. It's one way of exploring a world you've never been a part of. It's the joy of writing, of creating. You find a different world that way."

A slightly less cheery if just as pragmatic view is advanced by Amy Holden Jones, the extraordinarily versatile editor-turned-writer-turned-writer/director (though, like Anderson and Allen, she says she could live without directing because it takes a year and a half out of her life, but she could never live without writing). Jones, born in 1953, studied art history at Wellesley College and still photography at MIT, where she got involved in filmmaking. A short, *A Weekend Home*, won a prize at a student festival and one of its judges was, luckily for Jones, Martin Scorsese, who gave her a job as an assistant on *Taxi Driver* and, a bit later down the road, also introduced her to Roger Corman, for whom Holden Jones edited until Corman gave her a chance to direct (and rewrite). Oddly enough, the film, *Slumber Party Massacre*, which Jones took some feminist flack for working on, was originally written by feminist darling Rita Mae Brown.

Jones was working as a union editor in Los Angeles (after trying documentary filmmaking but finding there was little money in it) when she got the call from Corman. She scoffs at criticism of her for writing and directing a film in which coeds were slashed—called a driller killer by some—saying she got through the writing of it by thinking of it as a kind of chick flick. Perhaps this toughened her up for the indictment of her script for *Indecent Proposal*, the 1993 film in which Robert Redford's character gives a husband (Woody Harrelson) $1 million to spend the night with his wife (Demi Moore).

People forget, says the attractive brunette, that "Martin Scorsese and Jonathan Demme cut their teeth with Roger, as did so many others in the business. And among the many valuable things Roger taught me was that you could make a movie about just about anything, as long as it had a hook to hang the advertising on.

"Anyway, I'm not an artist. Some screenwriters are, but I'm not sure there are that many in the film business, because it is a business. There may be more in the independent film world. An artist would put his own vision at the head of the project, and I try to fit my vision into the project; I try to make them work together." Indeed, it *would* be hard to find a vision, or make a case for Jones, as successful as she may be, as an auteur: her work also includes *Love Letters*, *Maid to Order*, *Mystic Pizza*, and the family comedy *Beethoven*. Still, she has said of her craft, "To make movies you care about, you should be able to write the script. Or at least rewrite it."

Love Letters, Jones's first original script, was made at Corman's New World Pictures for $600,000 and starred Jamie Lee Curtis. *Maid to Order*, the 1987 movie with Ally Sheedy as a Beverly Hills brat who becomes a Beverly Hills maid, was written by Jones with the goal of directing it. Though in retrospect she observes, "I wrote because I had to write to get a script to direct. Ultimately, it's become more important to me than directing. In fact, if I never directed again I'd be unhappy; if I never wrote again I'd be truly miserable."

Feminist critics were thrilled with *Mystic Pizza* because it was a "small" film about friendship among three young women in New England during a cusp year of their lives (and indeed it launched the career of Julia Roberts). But *Beethoven* was taken to task because the wife in the film didn't want to work (Holden Jones says that she felt it was the woman's choice, probably a more tenable slant currently). They went bonkers, of course, over *Indecent Proposal*, in which Woody Harrelson is offered a million dollars to "let" Robert Redford sleep with his wife.

Jones was directing low-budget movies when *Mystic Pizza*, which she wrote, became a big hit in 1988. "I thought to myself, 'I didn't direct it, I wrote it, so why don't I try to write a big-budget movie with big stars that someone else would direct?' I thought maybe that would get me some currency, some power. That's how I came to write *Indecent Proposal*.

"When you write for hire, producers or studios come to you with a take and you dream up the characters and the story. In that case there was a book from which they took just one line: 'couple goes to Atlantic City and meets a man who offers them one million dollars for a night with the wife.' "

In her first draft, Jones cast the couple as a working class duo who went to the millionaire but couldn't go through with it, and the millionaire fell in love with the woman anyway. It was more a script about trust, she says, and it definitely worked. But the studio wanted a glitzier couple, and Redford didn't want to be in the position of being rejected.

"If you write for any studio, even if it's an original script," says Holden Jones, "you have to be prepared to change it. I think that's one of the biggest problems that stops a lot of screenwriters. They can't change it." Clearly, she is not among those screenwriters who insist on "maintaining their vision," with this logically leading them to feel they must direct their projects. In fact, Holden Jones says that very early on in her career she decided this would not be the route for her to take.

Overall, Holden Jones describes herself as an "ardent feminist," crediting parents who brought her up to believe she could do anything while still admitting (to Nancy Mills in the *San Francisco Chronicle* in July 1987) that "having children [two] slowed me down a lot. But I have no regrets. I love having kids. They've given me more pleasure than anything else." She is married to cinematographer Michael Chapman.

Realistically, she observed, "Ten years ago it was virtually impossible for a woman to direct. A woman might get one shot and then not be heard from for many years. Now it's easier for us to direct, but it's still very difficult to make movies women want to make."

One woman who is writing and sometimes directing the kind of films she wants to make, but these days for television—and quite a change from her high-flying days of the 1970s—is Joan Tewkesbury.

She is still working and working hard in her sixties, and glad to hear stories about another "older" working woman writer (Jay Presson Allen, in her eighties). "Bless her heart for telling it like it is," says Tewkesbury of Allen the day I interviewed her in the Westwood section of Los Angeles next to UCLA. Tewkesbury, another veteran in the business, was happy to hear that someone was giving a true perspective about the movie business (see Chapter Two, "Vets and Lifers").

She also agrees with Amy Holden Jones's analysis about the need for flexibility in moving from writing to directing, and often back again. For instance, she says that the experience of writing and directing Faye Dunaway in the television movie *Cold Sassy Tree* in 1989 was both energizing and hands-on. Tewkesbury wrote the teleplay, adapted from the Olive Ann Burns book, and Dunaway stars as Love Simpson Blakeslee, a turn-of-the century Northerner who scandalizes a small southern town by marrying a widower only three weeks after his wife has died.

"I could adjust what I had written whenever I felt like it, and that is a great privilege, and works well for actors too. I always like to have their input, and it was terrific to be able to hear what Faye had to say." Faye Dunaway was also the executive producer for *Cold Sassy Tree*.

Yet while this privilege is not always possible, Teweksbury says she does not let this get in her way. For instance, though she did not do the scripts, it was still a delight to direct Keri Russell as a recent high school graduate in two episodes of *Felicity* in 1998: "Spooked," and "Drawing the Line." "I have daughters, and I let this inform my directing, or so I hope," observes Tewkesbury.

Tewkesbury won acclaim and achieved breakthrough success as Robert Altman's script girl and then screenwriter (for *Nashville* and *Thieves Like Us*). And she seems able to laugh off some buzz about her which put her in the "B" list of directors—that is, if you can't get Robert Altman you can always get Tewkesbury. "I'm glad to be mentioned in the same sentence," she says graciously and unflappably.

When we met to talk, Tewkesbury took a break from working in her home office in Santa Monica, where she was putting together a pilot for a series about a restaurant for cable television's Showtime channel. It is a self-enclosed world in a box, she says of the story line, acknowledging the similarity with *Nashville* (1975), the Altman film with a huge ensemble cast, major stars, and a plot which explored and explained the country music scene in Nashville. The influenced film is credited with inspiring Allison Anders's *Sugar Town* in [1999], set in L.A. Of her pilot, Tewkesbury said "All the activity is about people in one room, a dining room, but they are people with lives that continue outside the box.

"Restaurants are an arena second only to show business with pressure-cooker environments. And it's like show business in that you have to make a presentation, only you have to deal with the food, too. It's really incredibly complicated."

This sense of fullness, of lives that "spill," fits what she and Altman developed together: the overlapping dialogue and multiple narrative line, which early on became his trademark. (This "innovative" technique has been imitated by many others, including David Mamet in this writer's opinion. Other critics date this technique back to Howard Hawks in his pre-1960s films.) Tewkesbury said that this sense of life and language going off in all directions was a form created as she worked with Altman on the set, every day.

Through a mutual friend (the actor Michael Murphy), Tewkesbury had met Altman and told him she also wanted to direct. His advice to her was to first become a script girl, which she did for *McCabe & Mrs. Miller*. "He told me it was the worst job on a movie set, but it was the best way to learn all about the film business. You learn who does what, what the demarcations and spatial locations are all about. Plus you see how well it works when an actor—anyone, really, working in this collaborative way—is truly generous. That is, when there is a wonderful exchange of energy back and forth. That's when things really get creative, and the energy flows."

Tewkesbury knows about acting. That's one of the ways she entered the movie business. Originally from California and a middle-class background (her mother was a nurse, her father worked for the Board of Education), Tewkesbury says: "Like a lot of women my age, my mother wanted me to be Shirley Temple; she had wanted to be a dancer, though she was a nurse. She was kind of lost at the movies, and sent me to dancing school." This was one of the reasons her family moved to Los Angeles, where Tewkesbury studied dancing with the Cansino Brothers (uncles of Rita Hayworth) and with Ernest Belcher, another famous dance instructor and father of Marge (of Marge and Gower) Champion.

The teenage Tewkesbury was the exact height and weight as Mary Martin, and her first official theatrical job was as an understudy in *Peter Pan*. She also realized she could "make some good money" as a dancer, and this was her initial entry into the movie business. However, she reminisces, "I found the mechanics of movie making— looking at the crane and seeing how a movie is put together—more intriguing than trying to get your dance steps right."

Tewkesbury ironically observes that she is of a generation that had three career options: become a secretary, a chorus girl, or get married. "Though the main idea was first, you would get married, and then do other things." But show business seems to have had designs on Tewkesbury her entire life, though she did indeed eventually marry and have a family.

She says that the idea of a self-enclosed box—one of her theories moviemaking—was there from the start. "I was intrigued by the idea of a pattern or structure, which is the essence of movement on the floor, being captured in a box. A movie is a box like that, though finally I became fascinated with the idea of how lives, and dialogue, spill outside that box."

Ultimately, Tewksbury graduated from dancing to directing, both in New York and Los Angeles, and had her own theatrical troupe which annually went to the Edinburgh Festival. "When you direct, you pull energy off the people you are working with." Eventually, Tewkesbury found her way back to California, and while there saw the movie *M*A*S*H*. "I saw right away that Altman's concept of working was much the same as mine. Nothing ever stopped. Altman's stuff spilled. My stuff spilled. Movies are not all perfect." Through a friend—Michael Murphy, an actor Altman has often used—she met with the director, and after becoming a script girl at his suggestion, eventually started writing with Altman, first as cowriter with him and Calder Willingham for *Thieves Like Us*, and then for Altman's stylistic breakout film, *Nashville*, in 1975, as the sole screenwriter.

As of this writing, Tewkesbury lives in Santa Monica, and has a house in New Mexico. "I find it necessary to get away from a town where there is nothing but movie talk, and to see how 'real people' are sometimes," she says. Wearing a black (de rigueur in L.A., it seems) pantsuit, with two pieces of very good Bakelite jewelry, Tewkesbury has short, cropped blond hair. She is divorced from her husband, who she says was in a high-risk business, though not the movie business.

Her first writing-directing debut was *Old Boyfriends*, a movie which—when it came out in 1977—was a minor feminist victory. "We were the three Joans," Tewkesbury says as the press dubbed her, and two other writer-directors named Joan, "Me, Joan Micklin Silver, and Joan Darling. We were lumped and dumped. When that happened, I saw the handwriting on the wall and went into television work." In addition to episodes for *Felicity*, Tewkesbury has also directed *Wild Texas Wind* in 1991, *On Promised Land* in 1994, *Scattering Dad* in 1998, and *The Guardian* in 2001. She believes that much of the exciting and creative work in the industry is being done in television these days. "There are so many MBAs in the movie business these days and each one has to have their say in a script. I'm not saying they're not smart people. They are Yale, Harvard. But they're business people.

"In television there's a chance that a writer, or writer-director, will manage to keep a vision intact. You can get in and get out quickly enough that not that many hands will be involved."

Tewkesbury thinks (and clearly hopes) she sees a change in some of the young men she teaches. Though marketers have always aimed their blockbuster films at the target 14-year-old boys, which many feel has resulted in violent films and perhaps parallel real-life behavior, Tewkesbury senses her students may change after the events of 9/11. "There seems to be a movement now toward a more personal, visionary movie," she says of some of the work she is currently seeing at the Arts Center in Pasadena.

I interviewed her before Robert Altman made his widely quoted remarks about the movie industry—that the World Trade Center tragedy would not have occurred without the stimulation of huge, action-backed blockbuster movies. It is still interesting to note that he, with whom Tewkesbury worked, made similar if not identical observations about the cause and effect of movies and real-time events. He also expressed that he hopes this would be a wake-up call for the movie business, which would start making films about personal relationships once again, instead of encouraging violence. Indeed, his subsequent film *Gosford Park* may have been a working exercise in what he was trying to do; self-described as a "who cares who done it," according to his screenwriter Jullian Fellowes.

Tewkesbury's work schedule is a kind of non-schedule. Unlike a lot of writers who feel they work best in the morning, or need an office, she says she can work anywhere, at anytime. This day she graciously chose to break up her workday and drive to brunch at the W Hotel: a visual reminder she said of the pilot about the restaurant business she has been working on. "Serving food is a lot like performing. It's about coordination and presentation."

She also has a highly unusual practice for a writer these days: her first draft is always handwritten. "Because I was a dancer I find something kinetic about handwriting my work. I think it's a physical thing. I use legal pads. I send my work out to be transcribed, and I get it back the next day. It's like the elves did it."

Moreover—and this is the first time this interviewer has heard this approach—Tewkesbury works continuously on a first draft, with no act or scene breaks. "When and where to break is something that gets worked out on the job," she says, though it's obvious that this might be easier only if the writer or writer-director is actually present. (Nor, as one might expect, does Tewkesbury use or believe in any kind of scriptwriting programs, courses, or pro forma approach such as the seminars that are nationally popular.)

After a moment or two of hesitation, Tewkesbury gives a measured answer to the question whether or not women write differently than men, or are attracted to different topics. "I'm interested in the small detail of the episodic film. The everyday fascinates me, and I suppose that one could say that's feminine. By the small things. I wouldn't necessarily say that is the case for all women but it is for me.

"Of course we always speculate about the question why women are not writing action films or violent films. Girls growing up just don't seem that interested in those kind of movies. In any case, right now I think we're in a kind of strange time for all screenwriters."

These three—Joan Tewkesbury, Amy Holden Jones, and Jane Anderson—are writers who seem to let the work dictate the terms of their employment; they don't let theory, or a "should be" stance, get in their way. This is not to say they are unaware of women's issues, or have no integrity in their work. But it may in part explain why they have managed to move effortlessly (or so they make it appear) back and forth between features and television, managing to work decade after decade.

They also have a quality of calm cheerfulness. Perhaps this is just a front, but it works. For a business where many kvetch, this surely works to their advantage.

Chapter Eight

The Smaller Screen—TV: A Better Fit for Women?

In the early days of movies, the spontaneous interchange of roles often resulted in an easy exchange of energy and ideas. A script girl could become a writer who would be on the set making suggestions to the director. Perhaps in fact she *was* the director. Or an actor might ask a writer to change or add some lines.

No longer. Corporate control, union rules, the studios, and bureaucracy in general have obviated this for many writers, not just women. Writers haven't been welcome on the set in most cases, one of the sticking points in the recent Writers Guild negotiations. The issue has become so pressing that an entire seminar was devoted to the problem in the third "Film and Television Writers Forum," presented by the Writers Guild Foundation. The seminar is called "Run, Writer, Run: Making Your Film Outside the Corporate Culture" and is advertised this way: "It's not a game, a toy, a theme park ride or a sequel. It's just a great script. How does a writer bring innovative work to a mass audience?"

One answer seems to be: TV. In recent years, more than a trickle of talented writers has gone to television. Many are now working for Showtime, Lifetime, HBO, and various other movie channels. Still others go for eposodic television or a long form such as a feature film. Tom Rickman, for instance, who won an Oscar for *Coal Miner's Daughter* in 1980, has completely switched over to television, saying that far too many years are required to see a movie actually get made.

He has written, among others, the Emmy-winning *Tuesdays with Morrie* (1999) and *The Reagans* (2003).

Perhaps we were set up for this creative switch by the watershed *Murphy Brown*; as Diane English, the show's writer-creator said in partial explanation of the show's success, "We all had our inner Murphy." Not only did we have a role model of a successful, aggressive and sharp-tongued professional woman who also happened to become a single mother, but the show's writer/producer/creator was a woman. There even was an "image of a woman television writer" in 1966: Sal Rogers, played by Rose Marie, in the early *The Dick Van Dyke Show*. And though you might have had to be a media insider or a real fan to know this, there were three women writers of *Saturday Night Live*— Anne Beatts, Rosie Schuster, and Marilyn Miller—who managed in the late 1970s to get and stay on staff and write now-famous skits for Gilda Radner, Laraine Newman, and Jane Curtin. All this in an atmosphere where John Belushi declared frequently and volubly that women couldn't write comedy.

You might even get fancy and say that women writers are more adept with a form that has an aesthetic composed of (1) familiarity (we know the characters), (2) continuity (they're with us for at least a season), and (3) intimacy (the actors' faces and stories are in our homes).

Or you could take it from one who's been there. According to writer Suzette Couture, television writing is more open to women, more communal. "I have found women to be eager to please in general, more so than men," observes Couture. "Of course this has its down side. But it is actually good for collaborative work. You can see this more easily in writing for television, particularly with women writing for TV. You're able to have more impact. In writing features, for instance, a writer will rarely have any say after a first cut. And sometimes in features one writer will turn in a project to a studio and it likely will be turned over to another writer, their writer. The original writer will have no say in the final product, or what happens after that point. In writing for television, there is simply more opportunity for more note-giving, note-taking."

Couture, who lives in Toronto, has written more than a dozen features for television, including *Vinegar Hill* (2005), *The Book of Ruth* (2004) *Choice: The Henry Morgentaler Story* (2003), *Martha, Inc.: The*

Story of Martha Stewart (2003), *After the Harvest* (2001), *The House of Gucci* (2002), and *She Stood Alone: The Tailhook Scandal, Conspiracy of Silence* (1991). Impressively, she has her own Toronto-based production company, with her husband Pierre Sarrazin. And while she has written numerous miniseries for Canadian television, she also observes, "There's so few features being done in Canada I think it's shocking."

Couture is concerned Canadian television is drifting away from the challenging dramas of the early 1980s, which may explain why she has been so active in the American television scene. She did, however, manage to write *The Sheldon Kennedy Story*, the tale of the sexually abused hockey player, which aired in the fall of 1998, and the miniseries *Jesus* in 1999 (though as a practicing Catholic she says she had a tug of war with her conscience about working on this project).

A former actress who studied journalism at Carlton College in Ottawa, Couture's breakthrough script was *Where the Heart Is*, the true life story of a Canadian Indian who married an Army officer in the late 1970s and was expelled from her tribe when she tried to go back after the marriage didn't work out. She and a group of other indigenous women protested the loss of her legal status as an aboriginal. Their protest took the form of "sitting in" on the tribal elders; ultimately the United Nations took up their cause.

Initially, there was not that much interest in the idea, Couture says, so she used the idea as the basis for a magazine story in the mid-1980s. After that, the CBC got interested and picked up the movie for television.

Couture says she believes she had perfect two-part training for becoming a screenwriter. She studied journalism in college and after graduating got a job at a local newspaper. "But as a young reporter, I kept getting in the way, inserting myself. I realized I should start to do some acting."

In the 1970s, Couture says, there was a highly active "New Theater Scene" in Canada where she honed her skills as an actress. "If nothing else, it gave you confidence that you could do as well writing yourself. So I had the best two schools for screenwriting work: writing and acting. Writing is an obvious training ground, but acting helps you understand the audience, which has been invaluable. The audience is part of the process and I know what it's like to be on stage in a cold drafty room with only twelve faces staring at you."

The bilingual Couture, who is French Canadian, says she prefers to work in her native Toronto, though she does "maintain an office in the States" for her production company. Through her agent, networks or studios will contact her, usually after a project has been decided on. And then comes the process of research and writing, which she says takes about eight months on the average. At that point a draft will go to the powers that be, and they will perhaps come back with notes and suggestions, and then some back-and-forths. Couture emphasizes, however, that in her experience rarely is the work taken out of the hands of the original writer, something that frequently happens in feature films.

In the case of the movie about the Tailhook scandal, Couture was in the position of having to write the script under the stricture of a lawsuit filed against the military. Therefore, she was unable to directly interview the film's subject: the woman who filed charges for sexual harassment against West Point. Instead, she read and researched approximately 5,000 radio and print interviews, resulting in a highly praised television movie. Couture points out that her research methods were actually not that unusual, for many made-for-TV movies are about deceased people, requiring similar research.

Not documentary but not fiction either, or even the kind of "ripped from the headlines" approach of reality shows, this real-life based narrative is typical of what Couture says she likes about writing feature movies for TV. "It's the writer's connection to the characters. Which character's point of view the story's tack will take." This is what makes a movie unique, for if this is lacking, she believes, the project may as well be written by just about anyone.

There is the real pleasure from following through a project, being part of the final mix. "Maybe you aren't in complete control, but the writer gets some respect. In the feature film world the writer will rarely even get to see a rough cut and after that nothing.

"I feel the writer's point of view can be very valuable in the editing room as well, though that's a rare occurrence."

For all these reasons, Couture, like so many other writers these days, has set up her own production company.

Writing for television, says Couture, has its own structure with certain breaks built in for commercials and station breaks. Yet she feels television writing is far from formulaic. She even believes she can tell if a script has been written by a woman. "Of course men can write for women, I'm not saying that," observes Couture, "but I have come to believe there is a secret language of women, which speaks more directly to me. Sometimes when I watch a film I say to myself, 'Only a woman'— sometimes This Particular Woman—'would have written this.' "

Couture says she realizes that this is a dicey thing to say, and in a business sense too. "No woman wants to admit that. That we may be that different from men. Besides, if you say that you may be losing some work by limiting yourself that way."

Susan Rice is another woman television feature writer, a Detroit native and now a confirmed New Yorker. She agrees that women do indeed write differently. "It's softer," she says over breakfast in Pastis, a West Village restaurant in New York City. "I do believe women's writing is more concerned with an interior life, with relationships." She is not sanguine, though, about the type and caliber of movies being written for television in the current popular trend of reality based programming. "It's simply cheaper for studios and stations," she said.

Rice has herself written movies for television in the "ripped from the headlines" mode. Her *When Andrew Came Home* is a reality-based film about a woman whose son is kidnapped—when he returns home after a five-year absence she finds he had been abused. Other work for television includes a segment in the series *The Lot* and made-for-television movies *For Hope* (1997), *A Match Made in Heaven* (1997), *Opposites Attract* (1990), and *Something in Common* (1986). (She has also written full-length feature films: *Enormous Changes at the Last Minute* in 1983 and *Animal Behavior* in 1989. Still maintaining her 310 area code even though she lives in Manhattan, Rice believes these features came about because she was then living in California.)

Rice graduated from Smith College with a degree in philosophy, and then took an M.A. in literature at the University of Michigan. Uncertain about what to do with those degrees, she came to New York City and landed a job at the Motion Picture Association, which had a magazine that reviewed films. "I went to exhibitors' meetings and was paid for seeing movies. That was for about three or four years, and

I also ran a Children's Film Theater for the next three years, giving tours to church and other groups. I was writing criticism on the side, for the Canadian film magazine *Take One*."

At some point Rice says she was at a screening and in a kind of flash moment thought to herself, "I could do that well."

Rice had saved about $3,000; she quit her job, and went to Martha's Vineyard on a motor scooter with the sole intent of writing a script. "It was April 8 and I left on June 20 with a finished script, just as the tourists were coming to the Vineyard." In November of that year Jane Fonda optioned the film, called *Love 30*, for $10,000.

"It was a lot easier in the early days to get access to people," Rice says. "If you wrote something and someone liked it they would get it to someone. It was in the 1970s, and before all the protection. Now you have to go through a barricade of people to get someone to read something."

Love 30 featured a tennis star questioning some of her career and life decisions. Jane Fonda wanted the film changed to include a conflict with a multinational corporation. The movie never did get made, but the early success gave Rice the impetus to try to write full-time. "I thought, 'Oh, this is easy.' And it was never that easy again."

Rice also says this first experience also brought her up against what she calls the "friend-like substance" of the film industry. "Fonda had been out of town," Rice says, "and when she called me when she got back, I said, 'Oh, I'm glad to hear from you,' and she said very coolly, 'It's good to be back.'" Almost as if still trying to figure out the intensity of her reactions, Rice says, "The film industry is a business, yet you're dealing with something personal, something emotional. It's a hard thing to learn. I still haven't. After all, every pitch is something you care about. Or should."

Rice works at home, in a home office. "I have six feet of scripts on my bookshelves that I've written and in most cases rewritten three or four times. But I can't say I have a strict schedule. It's more like spending most of the day trying not to write and when the anxiety becomes too crippling then I write," she laughs. "It's really about working all the time," she says, "even when you're not at the computer."

She does have a very interesting theory about the mechanics of scriptwriting. "I like to do an outline first. Outlines are confidence builders. But the truth is you have to write about twenty or thirty pages before the characters come alive. And then the script becomes character driven. Then around page eighty or ninety you start to think it's terrible. You feel you have to go back and redo the whole thing. Then you go back, maybe get stuck, do a kind of rewrite and by then the last twenty or thirty pages kind of finish themselves."

Rice says she believes the ability to write dialogue is a God-given gift; you simply have to have an ear for it. But you can learn structure, mainly by doing it. "When I wrote my first script I didn't know anything except what I'd picked up by going to the movies. The first actual screenplay I saw was for *Butch Cassidy and the Sundance Kid*. But you can do worse than picking up Bill Goldman [the scriptwriter for *Butch Cassidy*]. At that time I kind of imitated what I saw in print, on the page." She adds however that she could never do what Goldman does, what she calls a kind of pitch within a presented script—that is, hyperbolic descriptions of the action.

"I've written features for twenty years. And I've worked with estimable people like Norman Jewison, John Avildsen. I've even produced a full-length theatrical film, *Animal Behavior*, though it took ten years to actually get made and released." One of her favorites seems to be her movie for television, *Something in Common*. "It's a movie about a woman with a son who is dating someone her own age." The idea was suggested by a producer friend she ran into while crossing the movie lot at Universal Pictures when visiting L.A. once. But Rice cautions that "it's the kind of film that could never get made now. I like to think TV movies are in transition rather than being dead. But the truth is the TV feature movie is out of fashion at the moment."

She has come to believe that at one point advertisers felt that women were the market, were buying things they saw advertised in the ads accompanying television movies, particularly "jep"—women in jeopardy—films. But that is no longer the case. If there is a feature film audience to be appealed to, it is thought of as young men between eighteen and twenty-five who go to movie theaters.

Instead, now, she says that "reality shows" are cheaper to make and produce. "The question is, how long will people want to watch reality shows?" CBS, she points out, is the only major network that consistently has a Sunday night movie. None of this bodes well for writers of movies for television. While cable may be one obvious and viable alternative, there are economic drawbacks to this route [for success].

"If a movie is rerun on a major network, the residual will be $30,000 for a writer. But that's simply not the case with cable." At the time of writing, Rice was in the stage of waiting to hear about her projects. She said she had two scripts she had written for the networks, and what generally ensues is that after a period of several weeks, maybe months, notes will come back with a reaction or suggestion. "I'm waiting to see if I have a future in the business," she says ironically.

One "reality-based" movie for television that Rice enjoyed writing was *Tears and Laughter: The Joan and Melissa Rivers Story* (1994). "I love Joan. She's so honest. And really quite generous. I said to her, 'Why are you doing this movie? Why reveal the most anguished period of your life?' She said, 'Because Melissa needs the tape.'" Melissa, her daughter, needed an example of work to show to get more work.

Rice says she does believe that men and women write differently. "Women are more concerned with emotional issues, with an interior life. We simply have a different sensibility than men. I think at this point it's safe to say that we are different sub-species.

"It's an extreme example, but for instance I really don't believe *Sex and the City* was written by women. I've never seen women behave that extremely as sexual predators. It's more a gay man's idea of what women are like.

"They say women don't like action movies and men don't like films about relationships. I wouldn't go that far. I like *The Terminator*. I loved *Silence of the Lambs*. But I just don't want to see the mechanical robot thing any more."

Here are two somewhat different views of the experience of being a woman writer of feature films for television. It is the Canadian Couture who feels that women's writing is different from men's, and particularly appropriate to television writing.

The statistical facts about the gender gap between male and female writers has been studied by the Writers Guild of America:

From 1991 to 1997, women writers' share of employment barely changed. Male writers outnumber female writers by about 5 to 1 in feature film and by 3 to 1 in television. In feature film, there has been virtually no change in women's share of total employment since the early 1980s, and in television there has been little change since the early 1990s.

Throughout the 1990s, the gap in median earnings between women and white males was generally narrower than it was in the 1980s. Throughout the 1990s there has been a consistent gender disparity in median earnings among television writers, and in every year but 1993 among film writers. Among television writers, the gender gap in median earnings narrowed substantially in the 1990s and was just 5 percent in 1997. Overall, considering feature film and television work combined, the gender gap in median earnings has ranged from 10 percent to 15 percent in each year from 1991 to 1997, compared to gaps ranging from about 25 percent to over 40 percent for most of the 1980s.

Overall, there is substantial variation in women's representation among those who received credits on episodic series during 1997–1998). Among the series with no woman or just one woman among those who received on-screen "written by" "teleplay by," or "story by" credit were *Brooklyn South*, *Something So Right*, *Politically Incorrect*, *The Tonight Show*, *Seinfeld*, *The X-Files*, *Frasier*, and *Jag*. Among the series on which women accounted for 50 percent or more of the credited writers were the sitcoms *In the House*, *Moesha*, and *Sabrina, Teenage Witch*, and the dramas *Profiler*, *Party of Five*, and *Touched by an Angel*.[1]

As one might expect, most American women writing for episodic television are centered in Los Angeles and say this is required for them to make headway in the game. Three who have broken in—Melissa Rosenberg, Marti Noxon, and Susan Dickes—are an elite grouping with a complicated structure of personal relationships and professional interconnections. In other words, they seem to know each other, either through working together or other industry activities. Rosenberg especially is highly active in the Writers Guild of America West, seems to know everyone working today, and—a rarity it seems in any writing business—is quite generous in giving out contact information for other writers (with their permission, of course).

To a woman, the three agree that one must be in Los Angeles to make it in television episodic writing, if nothing else for the contacts and the need to be on hand for the frequently studio-based locations of weekly meetings of writers.

Melissa Rosenberg has worked on *The O.C.*, *Party of Five*, *Boston*

Public, and *Dr. Quinn Medicine Woman*. Marti Noxon was the chief writer for the extraordinarily popular *Buffy: The Vampire Slayer*. And Susan Dickes has made it into the nearly exclusively male bastion of comedy writers, including shows such as *Just Shoot Me!*, *The Drew Carey Show*, and *Mad About You*.

Like a lot of women who have come into the business in the past decade or so, Melissa Rosenberg had a clear game plan for breaking into the industry.

Originally from northern California, Rosenberg went to Bennington College and studied dance and theater. After deciding that a dancing career was not in the cards for her, she decided to focus on the writing side of the entertainment business and entered USC's prestigious M.F.A. program, the Peter Stark Producing Program for Film and Television, to learn about the business side of the business. She was one of six women in a twenty-five-person program. When Rosenberg graduated, a woman who had also gone to both Bennington and the Stark Program—Liz Glotzer, President of Castle Rock Entertainment—and Stark Professor Glen Adilman put Rosenberg in touch with an agent. Even so, Rosenberg was working as a secretary when she got her first feature assignment.

Though that first feature was never made, it exemplifies what Rosenberg says is one way to get into the business. "Find a way to live, if you're not independently wealthy. Have some life experience. Know how to type. If you can, get a job as a writer's assistant so you can find out how things are done, and be on hand if something opens up. If you can't get a job as a writer's assistant—which are hard gigs to get—get a job as a literary agent's assistant. It's a brutal job that will kill your spirit. But you will form relationships with people in the business. Take scriptwriting classes at UCLA or AFI. And all the while keep writing. Then somebody may give you a shot."

Though Rosenberg says she is a character-driven writer who prefers to work on shows where shades of character are to be explored, she has learned to be flexible. She has written westerns and sci-fi. Surprisingly, she says she didn't really like *Dr. Quinn Medicine Woman*.

Above all, she really seems to understand the business, and is highly active on the Board of Directors for the Writers Guild. "There's politics in everything—the politics on a show are more intense," she admits. "The world is so small. It's a small intimate ride." Yet while this sounds a bit opportunistic, Rosenberg was one of the nicest women writers interviewed for this book. Perhaps she was also the one most honest about admitting to the real character of the movie industry today.

She describes the daily life of a writer—when a show is being made—with high excitement. "The person running the show is a show-runner. There are a number of writers he or she is directing. Maybe about seven in a room. There will be a story breakdown with an outline of sorts. One person goes off to write up a story.

"It's like sending somebody out for an errand. Then you send somebody else out. But it's important to have some sense of what the show is about. That's the job of the show-runner. Or head writer."

According to Rosenberg, John Wells is one of the last great show runners, and he taught his writers how to run a show. "He really raised producers. Lydia Woodward is one of his people. You bring people up, so there's a seamless transition."

Rosenberg agrees with script guru Syd Fields's analysis that in movies there are three acts, but explains that in television there are usually four acts of seventeen pages each for an hour-long show. They follow the "teaser," which is three to six pages long.

When I spoke to Rosenberg, she had just returned from a trip to Baltimore, the setting for a feature she was working on. It was not a television movie, though. "I'm only 42 now," she says. "But there is ageism. Very few writers work after the age of fifty in the television business. It's a real problem." Nora Ephron says she has run into ageism even in features, however, and she talked about this with me during an earlier interview.[2]

For comedy writer Susan Dickes, the biggest problem is food. Too much of it, she says. And too wonderful. The pressures in the Writers Room are so intense that if a writer even drops a hint that a certain food item would be appreciated, an assistant will immediately supply it. The savvy-seeming Dickes is originally from the New York City borough of Queens and made her way to Los Angeles after graduate school at the University of Texas, where she got a degree in theater arts. She gives a self-effacing "mmmmmm" in reaction to a comment that perhaps being from the New York metropolitan area was helpful in her very successful scripts for *Mad About You*, the series about a newly married, dual-career, urban couple.

Like Rosenberg, Dickes seems to understand very well the "business" side of the business, and delights in talking about it. Doing a television pilot, for instance, is an intense experience that Dickes likens to a drop coming out of an eyedropper. Only one or two actually emerge from everything that is in the works.

"There are as many ways into the business as there are people working," she adds. "Some say get a job and be on hand. I've seen this work, but I've also seen people get stuck in support positions. Yet however a door is opened for you, it won't matter if you haven't got the goods," she says. "Even if you're somebody's niece or all the things they say about nepotism in Hollywood. You have to have your writing samples ready."

She says that she was constantly writing when she first got to California so she would be ready for her first big break, even writing jokes and scenes while she was in her car driving the seemingly interminable Southern California freeways.

The tutor/mentor system as described by Melissa Rosenberg is very much in evidence in the success of Marti Noxon. She was an assistant to Barbara Hall, who was instrumental in getting Noxon an agent. Through this agent, Noxon got a job on *Buffy the Vampire Slayer*, the hugely successful show on which she became a show-runner with Joss Whedon for the last two seasons. The show was so popular in fact that it had an active fan base on the Web, and Noxon would answer questions from time to time.

Buffy made creative use of two anti-stereotypes: the "bad girl," and the female as wielder of violence and revenge. She says she had no problem writing violent scenes, and doesn't see this as a "sex-linked characteristic" at all. Other credits of Noxon's are *Just a Little Harmless Sex* (1999), *Angel* (also 1999), and *Still Life* (2004).

Noxon was a theater arts major at UCSC, not to be confused with USC ("maybe I *should* have gone there," Noxon muses fancifully). But with her own office, an assistant, and an incredible busy schedule, she clearly doesn't mean it. When I spoke to Noxon, she was working on a pilot, *Point Pleasant*, for Fox.

Whether or not their shows actually make the cut and get made (or cancelled), these writers seem to take it in their stride. Like Jay Allen, they seem to accept the terms: they are getting paid, and they know the rules of the game.

In a few instances it is not necessary to be in California to write for television. For example, when a show is based in New York. One writer who has gotten media attention is Allison Silverman, who has written for the *Jon Stewart Show* and *Late Night with Conan O'Brien*.

Interest in Silverman's work, or in any case that of a female comedy writer, was so high that she did a week's worth of reporting on it for the Internet magazine *Slate*:

When I got to my desk this morning, my copy of *Our Bodies, Ourselves* was still open next to the anatomy book Adam gave me for its cross section of a vagina. Late yesterday, another writer and I worked on a women's health update for tonight's show. Though it's the first time we've tried it, we wrote the piece as if it's a longstanding segment: Women's Health with Vance DeGeneres. Hopefully, the concept of an earnest newsman landing the Women's Health beat will strike people as funny.

So, I saw *Our Bodies, Ourselves* lying open and thought I would write about being the only woman writer and about the composition of the writing staff in general. There's a widespread perception that being a female comedy writer means dealing with a roomful of Michael O'Donoghue wannabes who tell you "to be funny, you need a piece of meat between your legs" and then light your jokes on fire. No doubt, there have been awful experiences, but I haven't had them. No one's alienated me; no one's harassed me. I don't know why there are still so few women in comedy. Once I read that humor is an aggressive act. Jerry Seinfeld was quoted as saying, "To laugh is to be dominated." I think that's true; getting a big laugh is essentially forcing a person into an uncontrolled state. Though it's common to say that comedians just want an audience to love them, it may be more accurate to say that they want an audience to submit to them. I wonder if women are outnumbered in comedy because they're often discouraged from expressing aggression.[3]

Silverman went to Yale University and graduated Phi Beta Kappa in 1994 with a degree in humanities. While there, she was a member of the Exit Players, an improvisational comedy group. After college, Silverman became a part of Chicago's theater scene, but said that at the end of a year she realized that she did not want to become an actress. Instead, she became a puppeteer and then went back to comedy. She moved overseas to Amsterdam with BoomChicago, a theater organization focusing on slapstick comedy. "It was the first time I was able to make a living and perform and write," she said. "I lived by a leap of faith for a long time. It was tough to see my Yale friends making money and they seemed to know what they were doing."

Silverman eventually returned to America and began to submit comedic writing samples to television shows while living in New York City. Her work aired on *Who Wants to Be a Millionaire?* and she eventually landed a job at *The Daily Show* after calling the show's head writers, and then *The Conan O'Brien Show*.

Women writing for television today face the best and the worst of the screenwriting business. On the plus side, there may be more work, or product, out there, with more and more cable channels. But on the down side is the fact that television is even more youth oriented than feature films.

When I asked Rosenberg about this, mentioning the fact that perhaps more 40-, 50- and 60-year-olds (and beyond) are at home, and watching television, she explained that while this may be true, the television business is still run by advertising. Older audiences already have their brand loyalty in place, and so are written off by marketers. This is why a youthful writer is preferred for television.

Both Susan Rice and Melissa Rosenberg fussed that reality television is a factor that reduces the market for writers. Rice took the standard approach that there will be fewer shows to write if reality television keeps its stronghold, but Rosenberg took another tack. "It's unfair to try to cut writers out of that market," she says. "After all, somebody is still writing scripts for those shows."

There is also the wild card of TiVo, and no one seemed to be able to venture a guess as to its impact on the medium of television, or on the fate of writers for it. "The entire format of shows will have to be changed," Rosenberg predicted. Where advertisers used to be guaranteed a break every fifteen minutes for three ads in an hour show, that will all change soon.

Product placement is the only option for advertisers, and writers will have to learn a whole new format if the structure of episodic or feature television changes. (No more need for teasers, for example, to make sure the viewer comes back after the ad.)

When I countered that perhaps not all viewers will be able to afford TiVo, Rosenberg answered, "That's what they said about television too in the beginning."

Chapter Nine

The View from Abroad

To put some of the American screenwriting scene in perspective, it's useful to look at the situation for women movie writers working in other countries.

Though she very well may be—as she seems to both believe and assert, in a personally quiet but nevertheless not-to-be-ignored way—a law unto herself, Catherine Breillat is still in a good position to assess the position of women filmmakers in France. She has risen in her own county, pushing her way past numerous obstacles, to obtain a position of prominence. To not allow herself to go unrecognized.

"They *have* to deal with me," she says matter-of-factly, through her translator. "My films make money in France, and so I can't be ignored. Like everything else, it's market-driven."

As Breillat explains the overall structure, funding for films comes from a committee, which must approve a project. A certain percentage of ticket sales goes to the film industry, some to the committee, and some to the filmmaker.

Breillat adamantly points out that she is not "representative of France" though, and wants me to know that she is, creatively, very much her own woman. (Was there ever any question?) "I am enjoying some relative recognition and freedom now because I've reached a certain point of success in my work."

Breillat, in her early fifties, is a remarkably self-assured presence in any case. At the Mayflower Hotel on Central Park West for an interview the morning after her film *Fat Girl* had its American debut at the Lincoln Center Film Festival, her translucent blue eyes transfix you, almost like a cat's do—and, bypassing language (even though a translator is on hand)—she seems able to go to a nonverbal level, perhaps the actual intent or subtext, of interview questions.

In fact, Breillat is so far beyond worrying about pleasing others that her response to a question after the film's screening cuts off discussion: "It is the duty of art to take up questions of being politically incorrect. Therefore, I reject the question."

And even in the non-puritanical atmosphere of France, Breillat is a controversial filmmaker, having once made a movie, *Une Vraie Jeune Fille*, about a 14-year-old girl's sexual explorations, considered too explicit for her backers to release in 1975 (it did come out in 2000). Breillat confides that even during the making of *Fat Girl*, which has some outré sexual scenes involving underage girls, a couple of the people working on the film with her tried to keep the younger of the actresses who played Anais from having to perform a few of the bits in the script. Breillat is quick to point out that in any scene which included sexual shots, a body double was used for Anais. (And as if to further straighten out, or perhaps muddy, the issue, in 2004 Breillat made a film about the making of the film, called *Sex Is Comedy*, focusing on such "key" sexual scenes, and with the director being played by Anne Parillaud.)

Breillat reports that the French screening groups rejected the title *Fat Girl* for the film, mainly because it was an American term and concept, and so in France the movie was released as *A Ma Soeur*.

Fat Girl got generally good reviews and wide press coverage in the United States in 2001, and Breillat seemed pleased with the positive attention. Yet she never failed to punctuate her responses with the fact that she's French, no matter what reception she gets in other parts of the globe. Breillat is from a provincial area in the south of France, and from a middle-class family with no film connections. She and her sister appeared together as twins in Bertolucci's *Last Tango in Paris* in the 1970s (they are not twins, she points out, but look enough alike to be, which is what Bertolucci wanted).

Breillat's sister became a highly successful model, while Catherine Breillat stayed with filmmaking. Today, she admits that her sister is no longer speaking to her after *Fat Girl*, which has a telling and incisive narrative about two sisters: an intense examination of their love-hate, symbiotic relationship, and a conclusion even more shocking than the rest of the film.

"Just don't take no for an answer," is her answer to how to break through the barriers of getting a film made, particularly for women. "France is not the only country in the world where a woman director can make as much money as a man director," she points out.

While this may sound very familiar to readers of "how to" manuals for aspiring filmmakers in the United States, in one major way Breillat is very different. She says she will never develop a script around actors, no matter how much she has liked working with them or how fond she is of them. "I would never work that way, but instead let a story line or an image or an idea dictate the script," she says. "I very much liked working with Anais. And if it comes up, I would love to work with her again. But I would not write something with her, or anyone else, in mind."

An example of what you might call the fluidity of her script-to-screen process is seen in the evolution of *Fat Girl*. "Originally the script was more about Anais," she says. "But as the movie started being shot, it got to be more and more about the older sister." To this viewer, the film seems evenly divided between the two, though Anais, or the "fat girl," steals the picture.

In explaining why she changed the structure, Breillat says, "When you write a script, it's possible to project yourself onto one character. Whereas when you direct, characters take on a role by themselves. And when you're on the set as a director, it's important to be open, to reinvent." In *Fat Girl*, Briellat says that her actors were so much in character that Anais "felt unlovable." In the scene where she eats, as if in a mesmerized state, on a roadside stop, "She devoured those sandwiches with incredible voracity. It was absolutely strange and wonderful. I told her to stop but I think she could have eaten at least ten more, she was so much into that role.

"It was the same thing with the mother. She is not a smoker, but she chain-smoked throughout the entire film, just as her character does. That's the true way of being an actor."

Breillat says she never works from a strict outline. She writes at night, usually when she gets a burst of energy. "I don't use treatments; just go from a very vague idea and discover as I write. It's much more interesting this way than if you prepare everything in advance. It comes by itself. You don't have to rack your brain to find the right word."

Because *Fat Girl* has some scenes that deal with adolescent sex, Breillat says that the production manager tried to put some curbs on her as a director, worrying that Breillat was a pedophile. But, she says, "It is the moral obligation of art to not be strict or academic. That's the problem with being politically correct."

In fact, Breillat wrote a book about pornography after she finished *Fat Girl*. "I didn't know I was going to write a book. I had been very tired. But I couldn't stop myself from writing it. I wrote it in a month." (Breillat's first creative venture was a novel written when she was 17, *L'Homme Facile*.)

Her film *Romance* preceded *Fat Girl*. The first mainstream movie to feature an erect penis, *Romance* "scandalously" used real, not simulated sex. Breillat has said she considered the ironically-named film to be a kind of sequel to *Belle du Jour*, in that *Romance* explores areas of sadomasochism. While the attention given to the film may come from the sensational nature of the movie, it's also true that *Romance* is a film completely and totally taken from the point of view of a woman on a sexual quest: her boyfriend refuses to sleep with her, so she goes off to find her satisfaction and experiment as she will.

Though Breillat has been quoted as saying there is no distinction between a male or a female direction of a film, she still has some very strong statements about women's position in society. "What we hear a lot of now is men asking women: 'What else do you want? You've got all the rights.' First of all, I don't have all the rights. If I consider myself as a woman, that is to say universally, I look at a lot of countries where I have no rights. The freedom of women is very fragile—it has only existed for 20 or 25 years."[1]

As dedicated and as indomitable as Breillat may be, and though she may have been at times at odds with some elements of the film business, there do seem to be advantages to working in France. The film business is funded by an official agency as described above. But her individual films are also backed by a large company which guarantees a wide distribution, regardless of how they are received. Therefore, no panic about the opening weekend box office returns. And finally the French government puts a tax on each film, which represents half of the cost of the ticket to a movie. This tax is used to fund other films in France.

On the creative side, "In France," says Breillat, "movies, and therefore directors, go under a copyright law—the author law—and the producer has no right to interfere with any content decisions." Many (if not all) American screenwriters and writer-directors would be delighted with such a situation.

Breillat's slightly younger compatriot, Agnès Jaoui, whose film *Look at Me* opened the New York Film Festival in 2004, has a similar approach to Breillat's writing method, something that also sounds a lot like Sofia Coppola's method. Answering the question of the evolution of her scripts, Jaoui says she begins with the idea of how to say something original. It may be a character, or an actress, who inspires her. "Sometimes it will be a series of questions, and little by little a story is formed. After eight or nine months I will start to write dialogue. Sometimes after a social event, I will take a note, or write down a line."

Perhaps because they don't have to buck the difficult Hollywood machine, or crack the studio moneymaker code, neither Breillat nor Jaoui feels the need to turn to script coaches, formula plot forms, or even rigidly stick to a highly disciplined work schedule. It is art as well as business. And it is, clearly, character or idea driven.

The attractive, red-haired Jaoui answers what has obviously become a familiar question: "I don't mind being compared to Woody Allen, and his urbane world of sophisticates. But I don't want to look like him. These are my own films." And she insists that her co-screenwriter and husband Jean-Pierre Bacri (whom she directs in *Look at Me*) "is funnier than me." Jaoui started in the movie business as an actress in movies and the theater, and she has written—with Bacri—the scripts for Alain Resnais' *Smoking/No Smoking* and *Same Old Song*, as well as Cedric Klapisch's *Un air de famille*. Her first feature as a director was *The Taste of Others* in 2000. The couple is considered the most important screenwriting partnership in France.

The support for the independent voice or vision of a filmmaker is as strong, and more overt, in Australia and New Zealand. And there is a deliberate effort to propel women in the film industry.

Australia's most prominent and well-known female filmmaker is

Jane Campion, a current resident of Sydney though she was born in New Zealand. (Gillian Armstrong is also well-known, though she is exclusively a director [and not as much of a public figure as Campion], most recently of *Charlotte Gray*; also *Oscar and Lucinda*, *Little Women*, *Mrs. Soffel*, and *My Brilliant Career*.) Campion met one of her frequent collaborators, cinematographer Sally Bongers, when they were students at the Australian Film and Television School. "I think Sally's (the cinematographer for Campion's film *Sweetie* as well as *Peel* and *A Girl's Own Story*) a bit of a poet in her own right," says Campion. She met Bridget Ikin, producer for *Sweetie*, there too; Ikin was the producer for the innovative and critically acclaimed *An Angel at My Table*, the story of novelist Janet Frame.

Campion has always worked with what are now seen as women's themes. Her very first student film, *Tissues*, had the rather self-conscious—maybe even gimmicky—image of a tissue used, and featured, in every scene, side by side with a plot of a man arrested for child molestation. She says that the experience of making that Super-8 film left her "mad with the obsession" for filmmaking. Since that time she has done numerous female-centered movies, including *Sweetie*, *An Angel at My Table*, *In the Cut*, and her Oscar-winning script for original screenplay for *The Piano*, a film starring Holly Hunter playing a nineteenth century mute who travels to the bush of New Zealand for an arranged marriage and, instead, is liberated by erotic passion. Another example of a strong heroine can be found in Campion's film, *The Portrait of a Lady*. Campion's description of Isabel Archer determines, "She's a flawed heroine in the sense that she's a truth seeker and she's concerned in a naïve way about whatever her destiny means to her. She says, 'I don't intend to marry. I don't want to be a mere sheep in the flock.' She has that kind of arrogant conviction that she's worth more than most, and she's been told so."

Campion has said she likes being a filmmaker because it is people-centered work. "One of the most important things is to participate in relationships and friendships and particularly in the mythology of love. I have a deep need for intimacy. Almost every human being has it, and how you reconcile that with everything else in your life is a problem that comes up. Isabel denies its power to such an extent that when it hits her, when it's calculated in the way that Osmond (the fortune-hunting bounder played by John Malkovich) does, she falls for it in a devastating way." The same observation might be made of Ada, the heroine played by Holly Hunter in *The Piano*, who is also nearly done in by passion.

Sweetie, An Angel at My Table, and *Holy Smoke* all have heroines who find or are forced to release their true natures, generally at odds with their cultures. While this sounds like one of those formulaic dicta of screenwriter classes—protagonist against society—it's revealing that the female rebel/chameleon hero is a motif which runs throughout all of Campion's work.

Nevertheless, much of Campion's movie work has been supported in an economic and cultural way by her adopted Australia (she now lives in Sydney). Early in her career, Campion received help from the Australian Film Institute, which subsequently gave her filmmaking awards, and these days generally refers to herself as an Australian writer-director, though in fact she was born in Wellington, New Zealand. No direct relationship can be proven, of course, yet Campion's work seems strongly connected to her native land, though she does periodically disavow this. In a self-deprecation typical of New Zealanders, she told a writer for the *Toronto Sun*, who had made a tentative connection between Campion and the melancholia of the three main characters in *The Piano*, "Good Gawd, talk like that is such foolishness." Yet in another interview she told Douglas Rowe of the Associated Press, "New Zealand's a great place and they love to hate their creative people. My New Zealand heritage has made me afraid to show passion to a degree. It's very much a 'don't-get-so-excited' kind of culture. And I'm envious of those people, and respectful of those people whose passion is expressed in their work."[2]

A staffer at the New Zealand Film Commission defined that country's mindset as a "tall poppy syndrome" when I spoke to him about Campion and the film industry in New Zealand. When a poppy gets too tall, he explained, it is cut down, and this is the general attitude toward people who become successful. It is part of the national temperament of reserve and modesty that may be traced to the British roots of the country, but also to the large percentage of Danish and Dutch immigrants.

Campion recognizes this, characterizing it as, "You're a good girl, but don't go thinking too well of yourself."

Until recently, New Zealand had a history of losing creative people in a brain drain to other more exciting countries (though much of this is changing now that New Zealand director Peter Walsh's *Lord of the Rings* has been so successful). The truth is that New Zealanders do seem to have a very different character from adjacent Australia. The strong-willed and generally misaligned characters in Campion's movies may have more in common with the independent streak of Australians. Yet though the two countries are temperamentally different, both are consciously socially progressive, almost as if to make up for their colonial past. They share a commitment to alternative cultures and the position of women in general that is simply not to be found in American society. For instance, there is a society devoted entirely to the progress of women in "Kiwi" culture, called the "Women's Studies Association" with, of course, a website. Its announced goals are "to promote radical social change through the medium of women's studies. We believe that a feminist perspective necessarily acknowledges oppression on the grounds of race, sexuality, class and disability, as well as gender." Underpinning this is the recognition of the native culture, the Maoris. The next sentence is the kicker, especially when thinking about *The Piano*: "We acknowledge the Maori people. This means we have a particular responsibility to address their oppression among our work and activities."

For as quiet and reserved as New Zealanders may be, there is an ever-present recognition there of the Maoris, the tattooed and warlike people of Polynesian origin, significantly the only indigenous peoples in all of Queen Victoria's realm to have a legal, enforceable document with her granting them rights.

Obviously none of this was lost on Jane Campion. In *The Piano*, the adoption of Maori trappings by Baines, Harvey Keitel's character, is a strong part of the appeal of Ada's liberator/seducer, an outsider in his own homeland (of mixed blood, in fact, which makes things even more complicated).

It's this kind of tension that can be seen in all of Campion's movies. From her first early successful short *Peel* through *Sweetie* through *Holy Smoke*, the idea of not quite fitting in is central. Though it's easy to focus on her "difficult women," the iconoclastic theme is just as important.

Take for instance her use of the color orange, a leitmotif in *Peel*, which won Campion international attention and acclaim when first shown at the Cannes Film Festival. *Peel* follows an orange peel tossed out of the car of a family that happens to have red hair. The more rebellious and irritable nature of redheads, noted as far back as *Gulliver's Travels*, is one of *Peel's* themes.

While I know of no scientific study that supports these observations about, or Campion's use of, red-headed types as rebellious, it seems to have been observed in other cultures as well: Vedic medicine and philosophy, for instance, divides up people into three types, with Pita being the most excitable and high strung. Pitas are described as having red-hair, and a ruddy complexion. This is developed along slightly different lines in *An Angel at My Table*, where the frizzy, not-to-be contained hair of henna-haired novelist Janet Frame (or anyway, her stand-in) is presented as symbolic of Frame's unconventionality, the irrepressible nature of her talent.

It is that tension between societal repression and a sensuality beneath the surface which dominates Campion's interpretation of *The Portrait of a Lady*. In fact she has been quoted as saying of Isabel Archer's character that all women must get in touch with the part of their natures that yields to a strong male figure. Campion's screenwriter was Laura Jones, and their collaboration on this film was a very close one. Nicole Kidman, whom Campion chose for the part of Isabel Archer (then unselected and rehired), is a fellow Australian and perhaps not accidentally or coincidentally has red hair.

Holy Smoke was written by the Campion sisters and has a structure dependent upon the push-pull between breaking free and fitting in; it tells the story of Ruth (Kate Winslet), who has found her bliss in India but is "tricked" home to Australia by her family to be deprogrammed by guru-in-reverse Harvey Keitel. In an interview with the Australian Broadcasting Corporation, Campion said about *Holy Smoke* in 1999 that being celebrated [for her, as a filmmaker] "is just not a New Zealand thing to do. You know, I understand that. But in another way there's a depth to New Zealand appreciation of art in general which is quite moving—you know they won't clap in that kind of way that you might get in Australia, and I think that's a big reason why the Australian film industry has been so successful."

Commercially and critically less successful than Campion's previous work, *Holy Smoke* is structurally divided between the early awakening of Winslet by her guru in India, followed by her forced return to Australia and being reined in by her family. The twist is that she turns the weapon on Keitel's character: his seduction of her turns into her seduction of him, and this "feminist" spin—he falls hard for her, and she keeps her detachment—is a nice turnaround.

Still, *Holy Smoke*, as well as *The Portrait of a Lady*, was not as successful as *The Piano*.

One explanation is that the Maori motif energized *The Piano*. Campion believes, "in the [Maori] community, sexuality is totally out in the open, people talk continuously about their genitals"; she says she consciously used this to contrast with the repression of her protagonists. She has often spoken admiringly of the warmth of the Maori people, even wondering in public at times how they can "put up with" the cold and repressed Europeans who live in their country.

As of this writing, there is a newly successful wave of women screenwriters and filmmakers, often backed by the New Zealand government. Nikki Karo (*Whale Rider*) is one; Phillipa Boyens was one of three screenwriters for *The Lord of the Rings* along with the film's director Peter Jackson and his long-time partner Frances Walsh. This is Boyen's first script, though she was director of the New Zealand Writers Guild before being tapped to work on this film, because of her well-known love for and knowledge of Tolkien. Named by *Variety* as one of ten new writers to watch, Boyens has a strong awareness of the importance of women in film. After saying that Tolkien was often criticized for not writing great female characters, Boyens said in a phone interview: "We have a lot of differences between our female characters. They are very, very different from each other, which is wonderful as well. And the female energy in the film is very strong."

People in the American movie business just don't talk that way anymore, it seems. Depending on your bias, it may sound quaintly retrograde, or it may seem refreshing. (Female power base as a phrase is about as far as people will go currently.)

In addition to *The Lord of the Rings*, Walsh and Jackson wrote *Heavenly Creatures* in 1994, the debut of Kate Winslet in the role of one of two teens who plot to kill the mother of one of them. It was based on a real-life murder case in 1950s New Zealand. Exploring the intense love-hate feelings of the two young women, the movie was the first to bring international attention to the filmmaking duo of *Meet the Feebles* (1989), *Braindead* (1992), and *Forgotten Silver* (1995).

Jackson is always the director, though Walsh is also a board member of the New Zealand Film Commission and has mentored numerous women screenwriters.

The couple, described as lifelong partners, set up the National Film Unit, "New Zealand's only one-stop, post-production film processing laboratory." Some people credit them with the strong New Zealand film scene.

America certainly has its Robert De Niro, who founded Tribeca Film Center with its post-9/11 inspired allegiance to downtown New York. Producer Jane Rosenthal is a major operative within the Film Center, but it remains very much De Niro's enterprise, and vision.

Other than Campion, known primarily as a writer-director, perhaps the most well-known female screenwriter in Australia is Laura Jones, though Jones's reputation now seems to be an international one; she was picked for the adaptation of both *Angela's Ashes* and *The Shipping News*, both large and prestigious projects with no Australian connections.

Writing strong female parts in the United States is not something any female screenwriter seems to reach for or is well-known for these days: that description has been given, traditionally, to James Brooks, especially for *Terms of Endearment* and to Robert Benton for movies such as *Places in the Heart*, apparently a compliment and career builder if given to a man at a certain point in his career, but probably "career poison" if said about a female writer these days. There are two Women in Film offices in Australia, and one each in Toronto, Seattle, Los Angeles, and New York. In 1974, the National Film Board of Canada established Studio D, the only government-funded women's filmmaking group in the world, based in Montreal, and funding documentary films to be produced, directed, written, and crewed as much as possible by women.

Women's Film Festivals are at very least an annual staple in Australia and New Zealand. In New York City, where you might expect otherwise, there have been only two: one in 1978 when these issues seemed burningly important and novel, and one twenty-two years later. And though there is something to be said for not having government-funded arts (and it is said all the time when questioning funding to left-wing projects), it is still worth noting that the Australian Film Commission had an appropriation of nearly $30 million from the Australian government in 1997–1998.

Even more to the point is the fact that 38 percent of the films written in New Zealand are written by women. Observing that only 12 percent of films made in Hollywood are directed by women, though the figure is higher in the independent world. Debra Zimmerman, the executive director of Women Make Movies, the nonprofit New York-based film organization that has just celebrated its thirtieth anniversary, says that it's not that difficult to figure out: "The reason why women's cinema flourishes in Australia, Canada, France, even Iran is that they have governments that care about developing a national cinema. It's quite simple really. When it can happen, it does happen."

Some of this translates to exactly the kind of progressive images of women that many say they would like to see. *Variety* reporter Lisa Nesselson says of France today, "In the capital, a higher percentage of women (51.4 percent) than men (48.6 percent) comprise the filmgoing public. And—here's a surprise compared to the United States—the largest age group by far is filmgoers *over* 25 (62.2 percent), with a whopping 25.2 percent of them ages 35–49."

Observers also say that because the French film industry has continued to make a wide variety of pictures, people of all ages continue to go to the movies.

"Isabelle Huppert, Charlotte Rampling, Carole Bouquet, Kristin Scott Thomas, and other talents closer to 50 than 30 are constantly onscreen: middle-age women, far from being box-office poison, can be catnip for Gallic filmgoers."[3]

Possibly it takes someone who has actually worked on a woman's film to express the potentially broad appeal of women's films, across national and sex lines. Holly Hunter says, "I found it a very loving thing to read a script with such an unequivocal woman's point of view. And at the same time I don't think that *The Piano* is limited to being a woman's movie or that it's a woman's story. It's a humanist's story from the perspective of a woman, which is, I think, a very large thing to aspire to. And I think Jane was very successful with it."

Chapter Ten

Conclusion

The story of women screenwriters does not parallel the story of women film directors or producers, as compelling as those stories might be. In our time, and not to disparage those struggles, the fight for directorial and producing power has been an open, if a savage battle, as books such as Rachel Abramowitz's *Is That a Gun in Your Pocket? Women's Experience of Power in Hollywood* and Julia Phillips's *You'll Never Eat Lunch in This Town Again* have shown.

Today's narrative about women screenwriters is more ambiguous and multilayered. Therefore it is more difficult to assess, though perhaps a more interesing tale. Two parallels are working. Until very recently, writers in general, like women, had little control or power and made no organized or concerted effort to demand or gain it. They'd lost steam (according to some film historians) since the growth of television in the 1950s weakened the movie business and writers—iconoclastic by nature—weren't organized enough to buck the trend. It *is* telling that in the most recent round of Writers Guild negotiations even a unionized demand for "above the line" (or more prominently listed) credits on movies was considered extreme.

The second similarity is the more subtle fact that writers don't have to be seen to be heard. Like many of the positions women have traditionally held—in the movie business, for instance, editing was a job women got in on early and kept—writing is an anonymous, even faceless, position. (Even in the "modern" era, the now renowned Melissa

Mathison once found it necessary to write under the pseudonym Josh Rogan.)

Curiously, this has some advantages. Victim is not the word or status one wishes to assign, but in a number of ways being a second-class citizen may be something women have always been used to, and have learned to mold to serve their own ends. As Jay Presson Allen said, in reference to ageism, if "they" (executives who hired her to work) could see her, she probably wouldn't even be working now.

Though it's certainly a heterodox position to take in a politically correct world, female screenwriters may be more able to see an alternate route. Recently they are going in an underground railway fashion to the more open and "creative" venue of television (it used to be the independent film, but those lines have blurred somewhat) either by writing for episodic television or by doing quality work for cable. With the exception of Barbara Turner who still found that there were too many hands in or on the final product, a number of writers including Jane Anderson, Joan Tewkesbury, Suzette Couture, Allison Anders, and Susan Rice say they have more control over their work and are freer to do as they please in television.

A separate but connected issue is how women affect the roles they create, and add to the ways in which we see the world, and the Word. In her book *The Woman at the Keyhole*, Judith Mayne asserts "the difficulty of saying 'I' " for the woman filmmaker is far greater than for the woman writer. Yet if the cinema is symptomatic of alienation (novelist Doris Lessing) and reification (writer Christa Wolf), the attempts by women directors to redefine, appropriate, or otherwise reinvent the cinema are crucial demonstrations that the boundaries of that supremely patriarchal form are more permeable, more open to feminist and female influence, than these film-inspired metaphors would suggest. At the same time, it could be argued that the works of women filmmakers offer reformulations of cinematic identification and desire, reformulations that posit cinematic metaphors quite differently. The "difficulty of saying 'I' " does not necessarily mean that female authorship is impossible in the cinema, but rather that it functions differently than in literature."

Once again, as with writers in general, there is no clear consensus. About the only thing they all agree on, with the exception of the sweet-natured Alexandra Seros as well as television writers Marti

Noxon and Meredith Steihm (the co-writer of the original *CSI*), is that violence in movies doesn't interest them very much as writers, viewers, or women. (And Seros hedged by saying she is only attracted to violence when it is in the service of moving forward the action in a film.) Nor do most seem to care for the big blockbuster action movie.

Most writers shied away from the issue of sex differences in writing, but Foner, Rice, and Couture spoke of women's writing as being more interior, more about personal issues. Stacy Cochran said she believes women's writing for the screen, or hers anyway, may be characterized as "fluid," moving readily between an interior and exterior state, almost like a sleepwalker.

Suzette Couture was the only writer brave enough to say she could tell which woman had written a script just by seeing the film or reading the script.

One psychological underpinning for their positions can be found in Carol Gilligan's classic *In a Different Voice*: "Remember Piaget's observation, corroborated by Lever, that boys in their games are more concerned with rules while girls are more concerned with relationships, often at the expense of the game itself." Women are better team players, says Lucie Salhary, a television executive at United Paramount Network. This *should* make them a natural for the collaborative art of film. And the most recent stage of research in male-female sex differences has decided (for now) that even the developing female brain has a proclivity for verbal concerns, and the male's for spatial arrangements—and that women seem to use all parts of the brain simultaneously, and in a less linear way.

Perfect for the form of films, particularly "talky" relationship films. Not so perfect for narrative drive.

Yet Georgia Jeffries, TV scriptwriter for *China Beach* and *Cagney and Lacey*, begs to differ with these kinds of conclusions about sex differences in writing. When being told that she could write like a man with executives praising the "edge," the "passion," the "sharp dialogue and the occasional four-letter word," she found it laughable, observing that those in a position of power have now learned to be more careful. "In these politically correct times I find the executives no longer tell me I write like a man. Maybe they've learned that power and passion and active verbs have no gender (or class or race or national origin for that matter). Maybe not. I suspect that it is a daily battle still being fought by every writer who refuses to be limited or pigeon-holed. It does not really matter what "they" think after all. What I know is that I write exactly like a woman." Some of this echoes the earlier experiences of Leigh Brackett, who wrote scripts for Howard Hawks, and ultimately created John Wayne's characters in *Rio Bravo* and *Rio Lobo*. Hawks said of her: "She writes like a man—she writes good."

Though she did not respond to this compliment directly, she did say, at a conference at San Francisco State University, that Hawks' characters fit her writing syle so well because, "The women are all, by God, people, with independent lives and thoughts of their own, capable of being comrades and mates but always of their own free choice and as equals with men—an earned quality. Men have to earn it. So do they."[1]

And from the ameliorative point of view: Some writers, including Leslie Dixon, have asserted that they *intended* to write more progressive roles for women; and in the case of *The Thomas Crown Affair* even tried, unsuccessfully, to write a more ambiguous and realistic conclusion than the usual "off into the sunset" romantic happy ending. Audrey Wells said she worked hard to upgrade a "bimbo" part in *The Truth About Cats and Dogs* to give the character (played by Uma Thurman) enough self-esteem and native shrewdness to coolly assess and make use of her own value on the marketplace of men and marriage. Robin Swicord had similar comments about her re-creation of Amy March, a highly polished nineteenth-century sex object in *Little Women*. Swicord succeeded, she believes—with this project anyway—because Denise Di Novi was the executive in charge of production, and Gillian Armstrong, the director.

But others refuse to consciously put a female spin on characters: Amy Holden Jones, for instance, says, "I'll never write just politically correct. What does that mean? Women can be villains as well as heroes. What does that mean—that you can't write Lady Macbeth? Please! Blacks and women, we're complete humans, with good sides and bad. We make mistakes. If you cannot write the complex human who happens to be any one of those things, then you're not a writer; you've been hobbled." (Some say this is why the updated feminist interpretation of *The Portrait of a Lady* by writer Laura Jones and director Jane Campion did not work well.)

Yet overall, a stepped-up awareness of the importance of the screenwriter bodes well. When Russell Crowe accepted his best actor award at the 2002 SAG awards, he said "God bless narrative. God bless the story line." The televised Oscars that year showed actual script lines and pages on the screen when nominees were announced, a first in this writer's memory, and witty explanations of what an editor and makeup artist do were written by, respectively, writers Buck Henry and David Mamet.

In her acceptance speech for *Being Julia* at the Golden Globes in 2005, Annette Bening said: "Yes, it's true that there aren't that many roles for interesting, mature women. But it still is possible, if one is willing to fight for it."

Oddly, instead of gender difficulties, many women screenwriters seem more disturbed about a corporate culture that makes it difficult to make a film of personal vision or high quality. All the way from veteran professionals like Jay Presson Allen to the most personal of writers such as Allison Anders, a certain disaffection with mainstream moviemaking has set in.

In this way, women are reflecting what is by general consensus off-kilter in the movie business. "When I was starting out, they were still making movies in every price range," says producer Lili Fini Zanuck. "Now we have either this big tentpole extravaganza or a small movie." The independent film, difficult as it may be to finance and get off the ground, is turning out to be the main way for a moviemaker to create a film that has her or his own point of view. Filmmakers, including those who write movies—and in yet another permutation of art versus business—may have to accept the fact that they will either go the independent route, perhaps write for TV, or have their words changed by either a corporate executive or another writer, perhaps at the insistence of a studio executive.

The current bifurcation of small film versus the blockbuster sure thing, which will open big on weekends, has changed the movie business. It's not that women cannot write those big blockbuster films. It's just that many of them don't seem interested in doing so.

Something bad seems to have happened to the American movie industry, just as writers are pressing for more status and power, and women writers are trying to get in the door again and hoping to solidify their gains.

And one more thing about women screenwriters, the most obvious and therefore perhaps the most easily overlooked: with the exception of Allison Anders, Gina Wendkos, and possibly Lisa Loomer, nearly every woman writer I interviewed was from what Americans prefer to call the upper middle class; really our upper class. They were all from privileged backgrounds, or had gone to exclusive undergraduate or graduate schools. This may not be an observation that fits with what one would like to see—that is, radicalizing or changing at very least the form of film, or the images of women therein. But it is a fact.

Possibly this kind of background enabled them to network in the way that it is said one must do to make it in mainstream film and television. Perhaps a privileged lifestyle is required to pursue the making of independent personal films. Or maybe they were just well enough accustomed to go where the money is.

Appendix:
Brief Biographies of
Women Screenwriters

JAY PRESSON ALLEN

Born in 1923, raised in Dallas, Allen was the only child of well-to-do parents. She went to New York to become an actress in the 1940s, moved to Connecticut, and then to Los Angeles. One of her achievements was that she wrote a novel, titled *Spring Riot*. Allen divorced and remarried theatrical producer Lewis Allen and raised one child, Brooke Allen, who is the mother of twin girls. Jay Presson Allen lives in Manhattan and Italy.

Filmography: Thomas Crown Affair (1999); *Tru* (1992, teleplay aka *American Playhouse*); "Hothouse" (1988, TV Series); *Deathtrap* (1982, aka *Ira Levin's Deathtrap*); *Prince of the City* (1981, screenplay); *Just Tell Me What You Want* (1980, novel/screenplay); "The Prime of Miss Jean Brodie" (1978, TV Series); *A Star Is Born* (1976); *Funny Lady* (1975); *The Borrowers* (1973, TV); *40 Carats* (1973); *Travels with My Aunt* (1972); *Cabaret* (1972, screenplay); *The Prime of Miss Jean Brodie* (1969, screenplay/play); *Marnie* (1964); *Wives and Lovers* (1963, play *The First Wife*).

ALLISON ANDERS

Born in 1954 in Kentucky, to a secretary mother and bartender father. Her father disappeared when Anders was five. Gang-raped when she was twelve, Anders made gang rape the subject of her film, *Things Behind the Sun*. A teenage mother, she supported herself and two kids by waitressing and welfare in Los Angeles. Anders put herself through college when hit by the filmmaking bug; after writing a letter to Wim Wenders, he got her an internship on *Paris, Texas*. She lives in Los Angeles.

Filmography: Things Behind the Sun (2001); *Sugar Town* (1999); *Grace of My Heart* (1996); *Four Rooms* (1995, segment *The Missing Ingredient*); *Mi vida loca* (1993, aka *My Crazy Life*); *Gas, Food Lodging* (1992).

JANE ANDERSON

Born in 1954 in California, Anderson, a successful actress, appeared on Broadway before becoming a writer for television and feature films. Originally from Northern California, Anderson, openly gay, now lives in Santa Monica with her partner and child.

Filmography: Normal (2003, TV; *Looking for Normal*, teleplay); *When Billie Beat Bobby* (2001, TV); *If These Walls Could Talk 2* (2000, TV; segment "1961"); *The Baby Dance* (1998, TV/play/teleplay); *How to Make an American Quilt* (1995); *It Could Happen to You* (1994); *The Positively True Adventures of the Alleged Texas Cheerleader-Murdering Mom* (1993, TV); "The Facts of Life" (1984–1986, TV Series, writer).

CATHERINE BREILLAT

Born in 1948 to a middle-class family with no film connections, she grew up with her sister in the south of France. She published her first novel, *L'Homme Facile*, an erotic piece, when she was seventeen. She is highly regarded in France, and is well-known in the international film community, mostly for her controversial depictions of sexuality. Breillat lives in Paris.

Filmography: Anatomie de l'enfer (2004, aka *Anatomy of Hell*, novel *Pornocratie*); *Sex Is Comedy* (2002); *Brève traversée* (2001, aka *Brief Crossing*); *À ma soeur!* (2001, aka *Fat Girl*; aka *For My Sister*); *Selon Matthieu* (2000, aka *To Mathieu*); *Romance* (1999, aka *Romance X*); *Viens jouer dans la cour des grands* (1997, TV/screenplay); *Parfait amour!* (1996, aka *Perfect Love*); *Couples et amants* (1993); *Secret d'Elissa Rhaïs, Le* (1993, TV/adaptation); *Nuit de l'océan, La* (1992); *Thune, La* (1991, aka *Money*); *Sale comme un ange* (1991, aka *Dirty Like an Angel*); *Aventure de Catherine C.* (1990); *Diable au corps, Le* (1990, TV); *Zanzibar* (1989); *36 Fillette* (1988, novel, aka *Virgin*, UK); *Milan noir* (1987, aka *Black Milan*); *Police* (1985, story); *Araignée de satin, L'* (1984, aka *The Satin Spider*); *E la nave va* (1983, aka *And the Ship Sails On*, U.S.; aka *Et vogue le navire*, France); *Pelle, La* (1981, screenplay, aka *Peau, La*, France; aka *The Skin*); *Tapage nocturne* (1979, aka *Nocturnal Uproar*); *Bilitis* (1977, aka *Bilitis*); *Une vraie jeune fille* (1976, screenplay, novel *Le soupirail*, aka *A Real Young Girl*); *Catherine et Cie* (1975, aka *Catherine & Co.*, U.S.; aka *Letto in società, Un*, Italy).

JANE CAMPION

Born 1954. A second generation New Zealander, she received a B.A. in anthropology from Victoria University in Wellington, 1973. She traveled in Europe upon graduation, and later studied painting at Chelsea School of Arts in London. Attending the prestigious Australian Film, Television, and Radio School in the early 1980s, Campion met cinematographer Sally Bongers, with whom she would work later, most notably on *An Angel at My Table*, though she fired Bongers during the making of the film. Some critics say the film's visual quality deteriorated after that. She is married, with one child.

Filmography: In the Cut (2003); *Holy Smoke* (1999, aka *Holy Smoke!*); *The Piano* (1993, aka *La leçon de piano*, France); *Sweetie* (1989, screenplay/story); *After Hours* (1984); *A Girl's Own Story* (1984); *Passionless Moments* (1983); *An Exercise in Discipline—Peel* (1982, aka *Peel*).

STACY COCHRAN

Born in Passaic, New Jersey, she earned a B.A. in political science from Williams College, though Cochran once intended to write fiction. Her first feature, *My New Gun*, was made in less than one year after Cochran received her M.F.A. from Columbia Film School in 1992. She is married to an attorney, with one child, and lives in Greenwich Village.

Filmography: Drop Back 10 (2000); *Boys* (1996); *My New Gun* (1992); *Another Damaging Day* (1991).

SOFIA COPPOLA

Born May 14, 1971. Daughter of Francis Ford and Eleanor Coppola, she grew up in the Napa Valley and Manhattan. Married to director Spike Jonze, she is now divorced.

Filmography: Marie-Antoinette (2006); *Lost in Translation* (2003); "Platinum" (2003, TV Series, creator and story); *The Virgin Suicides* (1999); *Lick the Star* (1998); *New York Stories* (1989, written by; segment *Life without Zoe*).

SUZETTE COUTURE

A Canadian who studied journalism at Carlton College in Ottawa, she became an actress in Toronto in the highly active "New Theater" scene. Her own film production company is based in Toronto, where she lives. Couture is considered a major player in writing for the American television market.

Filmography: Vinegar Hill (2005, TV/teleplay); *The Book of Ruth* (2004, TV/teleplay); *Martha, Inc.: The Story of Martha Stewart* (2003, TV/teleplay); *Choice: The Henry Morgentaler Story* (2003, TV); *After the Harvest* (2001, TV); *Haven* (2001, TV); *Jesus* (1999, TV/teleplay, aka *Bibbia: Jesus, La*, Italy; aka *Bibel—Jesus, Die*, Germany); *The Sheldon Kennedy Story* (1999, TV, aka *Un rêve abîmé*, Canada: French title); *She Stood Alone: The Tailhook Scandal* (1995, TV); *Million Dollar Babies* (1994, TV, aka *Jumelles Dionne, Les*, Canada: French title); *Betrayal of Trust* (1994, TV/teleplay, aka *Under the Influence*); *Florida, La* (1993); *Child of Rage* (1992, TV); "Conspiracy of Silence" (1991, TV Miniseries); "Bordertown" (1989, TV Series, writer, aka "Deux font la loi, Les," France); "Road to Avonlea" (1989, TV Series, writer, aka "Avonlea"); *Love and Hate: The Story of Colin and Joanne Thatcher* (1989, TV, aka *Love and Hate: A Marriage Made in Hell*); *Blades of Courage* (1988, TV, aka *Skate!*).

SUSAN DICKES

Born and grew up in Queens, N.Y., she earned a degree in theater arts from the University of Texas. Now living in Los Angeles, Dickes has written and had plays mounted.

Filmography: "Just Shoot Me!" (1997, TV Series); "The Drew Carey Show" (1995, TV Series); "Mad About You" (1992, TV Series, writer); "Good Old Reliable Nathan" (1998, episode); "Mother's Day" (1998, episode); "Uncle Phil Goes Back to High School" (1999, episode).

CARRIE FISHER

Born in Los Angeles, October 21, 1956, this actress-writer is the daughter of Debbie Reynolds and Eddie Fisher. She attended Central School of Speech and Drama and made her professional debut as an actress at the age of thirteen in her mother's nightclub act. She had a small role in *Shampoo*, and is most famous for her acting role of Princess Leia Organa. An avid reader, she dropped out of high school at fifteen. Her marriage to Paul Simon took place in 1983; they divorced later. Script doctor for, among others, *Hook* and *Sister Act*, Fisher wrote the highly successful novel *Postcards From the Edge*, detailing what it was like to grow up as the daughter of a movie star, and has said that the novel started as a series of letters. She had a child with agent Bryan Lourd.

Filmography: These Old Broads (2001, TV); "Roseanne" (1988, TV Series);

"Arsenic and Old Mom" (1997, episode); *Carrie Fisher: The Hollywood Family* (1995, TV); "Carrie on Hollywood" (1995, TV Series, writer); "The Young Indiana Jones Chronicles" (1992, TV Series, writer); "Paris, October 1916" (episode); *Postcards from the Edge* (1990, novel/screenplay).

NAOMI FONER

She was born in New York in 1946. B.A. in English from Barnard College, M.A. in developmental psychology at Columbia. A member of SDS; she was Media Director for Eugene McCarthy. Foner worked in production at Public Broadcast Lab and Children's Television Workshop. Barbara Schults, head of the Vision series on PBS, encouraged her to write; she tried her hand with the "Blackout" episode in 1978. Married to director Stephen Gyllenhaal, she has two children: actors Jake and Maggie Gyllenhaal.

Filmography: Bee Season (2005); *Losing Isaiah* (1995); *A Dangerous Woman* (1993); *Running on Empty* (1988, writer); *Violets Are Blue* (1986); "The Best of Families" (1977, TV Miniseries, creator).

MAGGIE GREENWALD

Born in 1949, she grew up in Queens and Manhattan, while her parents were in graduate school at NYU. She attended the Performing Arts School, and went to film school at Los Angeles City College. Jobs included working as a professional driver, then film editor, before starting to write and develop her own projects. Greenwald lives in Brooklyn Heights with her husband, a composer, and their daughter.

Filmography: Songcatcher (2000); *The Ballad of Little Jo* (1993); *The Kill-Off* (1989); *Home Remedy* (1987).

AGNÈS JAOUI

From a Tunisian-Jewish background, Jaoui credits it for her iconoclastic outlook. Her father was a marketing consultant, her mother, a psychologist. She moved to Paris when she was seven years old. Trained as an actress, she met her actor-husband and writing partner, Jean-Pierre Bacri (thirteen years her senior), in 1987. Her directorial debut was *The Taste of Others*.

Filmography: Comme une image (2004, aka *Look at Me*); *Le Goût des autres* (2000, aka *The Taste of Others*); *On connaît la chanson* (1997, aka *Same Old Song*);

Un air de famille (1996, play, aka *Family Resemblances*); *Smoking/No Smoking* (1993); *Cuisine et dépendances* (1993, also play, aka *Kitchen with Apartment*).

PATTY JENKINS

A self-described Army brat, she lived all over the world while growing up. After studying painting and film at Cooper Union in New York, Jenkins moved to California and became a union cameraperson. She is a graduate of the American Film Institute Director's Program.

Filmography: Monster (2003); *Velocity Rules* (2001); *Just Drive* (2001).

AMY HOLDEN JONES

Born in Philadelphia in 1953, she studied art history at Wellesley College and graduated from MIT in 1974, where she studied photography and filmmaking. Her first feature film assignment was as production assistant on *Taxi Driver*, where Holden Jones met her future husband, Michael Chapman, a photographer on the film.

Filmography: Beethoven's 5th (2003, TV, characters, aka *Beethoven's 5th: Big Paw*); *Beethoven's 4th* (2001, TV, characters); *Beethoven's 3rd* (2000, TV, characters); *The Relic* (1997, screenplay); *The Rich Man's Wife* (1996); *The Getaway* (1994); *Beethoven's 2nd* (1993, characters); *Indecent Proposal* (1993); *Indecency* (1992, TV/story/teleplay); *Beethoven* (1992); *Saturday's* (1991, TV); *Mystic Pizza* (1988, screenplay/story); *Maid to Order* (1987); *Love Letters* (1984, aka *My Love Letters*).

LAURA JONES

An Australian, she enrolled in art school after high school. Her mother is a well-known novelist, Jessica Anderson. She started by writing scripts for Australian soap operas while being a stay-at-home mother. Considered one of the world's best movie adapters, Jones is a winner of Australian's highest honor, the AFI Byron Kennedy award. She lives in Sydney, Australia.

Filmography: Possession (2002); *Angela's Ashes* (1999); *Oscar and Lucinda* (1997); *A Thousand Acres* (1997); *The Well* (1997); *The Portrait of a Lady* (1996); *An Angel at My Table* (1990); *High Tide* (1987); "The Bush Gang" (1981, TV Series, writer); "Spring & Fall" (1980, TV Series, writer); "Cold Comfort" (episode); "Every Man For Herself" (episode); "Patrol Boat" (1979, TV Series, writer); "The Oracle" (1979, TV Series, writer); *Cass* (1978, TV); *Say You Want Me* (1977, TV); *Clean Straw for Nothing* (1976); "Certain Women" (1973, TV Series, writer).

CALLIE KHOURI

Born in San Antonio in 1957, she was raised in Texas and Kentucky by doctor father and mother. At Purdue University, she studied landscape architecture but switched to drama. She moved to Nashville after college to be with her family before heading to Los Angeles in 1982 to study at the Strasberg Institute, hoping to become an actress. She worked as a waitress, publicist for music videos, and in movie production before selling her first script. While working for a commercial production company as a receptionist before taking a position with it as a music video production assistant, Khouri started work on what would become *Thelma and Louise*. She wrote the script in longhand at home, then typed it on the job. Living in Santa Monica, she married writer-director David Warfield in 1990.

Filmography: Divine Secrets of the Ya-Ya Sisterhood (2002); *Something to Talk About* (1995, aka *Grace Under Pressure*); *Thelma & Louise* (1991).

LYNN HERSHMAN LEESON

Born in 1941, she is a performance artist and filmmaker, and lives in San Francisco. A professor at San Francisco State University, Hershman Leeson recently has had the first collection of her work curated: at the Henry Art Gallery, which describes her work and importance this way: "Politically expressed in drawings, paintings, photographs, performances, robotic works, digital art, videos, films, interactive multimedia installations, and artificial intelligence works, Hershman Leeson's project of self-analysis and self-mythification multiplies and refracts fictional identities though her artwork to the point of exploding any stable notion of identity."

Filmography: Teknolust (2002); *Conceiving Ada* (1997, aka *Leidenschaftliche Berechnung*, Germany); *Virtual Love* (1993); *Shooting Script: A Transatlantic Story* (1992).

LISA LOOMER

Born in 1950, she grew up in New York. Loomer lived for a time in Mexico and implied she was of Mexican heritage, but refused to go into this. Her plays produced on Broadway and regionally (best known for *The Waiting Room*). She lives in Los Angeles and writes for movies and television. Recipient of the Norman Lear Writers Award for positive portrayals of Latinos in media.

Filmography: Girl, Interrupted (1999); "Hearts Afire" (1992, TV Series, writer); "Room for Two" (1992, TV Series, writer); "Studio 5-B" (1989, TV Series, writer).

MELISSA MATHISON

Born in Los Angeles, June 3, 1950, she is the daughter of a Southern Californian journalist father and part-time publicist mother. Mathison attended the University of California at Berkeley, and was a stringer from San Francisco for *Time* magazine (a job she got through one of her father's contacts). Mathison connected with Francis Ford Coppola through her parents and reportedly had an affair with him. She married but is divorced from Harrison Ford, and has two children.

Filmography: Kundun (1997); *The Indian in the Cupboard* (1995); *Son of the Morning Star* (1991, teleplay); *Twilight Zone: The Movie* (1983, segment 2, as Josh Rogan); *The Escape Artist* (1982); *E.T. the Extra-Terrestrial* (1982); *The Black Stallion* (1979).

ELAINE MAY

Born in Philadelphia, 1932. Her father was an actor in Yiddish theater productions. She dropped out of high school at fourteen, but enrolled at the University of Chicago where she met Mike Nichols. Married and divorced twice to Marvin May and lyricist Sheldon Harnick. Mother of one child, actress Jeannie Berlin. May has lived in Chicago (Second City work with Mike Nichols), New York (Broadway successes with Nichols), and Los Angeles (writer and writer-director).

Filmography: Primary Colors (1998); *The Birdcage* (1996); *Ishtar* (1987); *Labyrinth* (1986, credited); *Tootsie* (1982, credited); *Reds* (1981, uncredited); *Heaven Can Wait* (1978); *Mikey and Nicky* (1976); *Such Good Friends* (1971, as Esther Dale); *A New Leaf* (1971).

MARTI NOXON

Born in California, this theater arts major at University of California at Santa Cruz graduated in 1987. Working with writer-producer Joss Whedon, creator and executive producer of *Buffy* and the *Buffy* spin-off series, *Angel*, Noxon was promoted from writer to executive producer and given charge of producing *Buffy*. After *Buffy the Vampire Slayer* became a hit, she was widely available to answer fan questions on her Web site. Marti Noxon appeared in the "Once More, With Feeling" episode of *Buffy* as a singing meter maid. She is married, with one child.

Filmography: "Point Pleasant" (2005, TV Series, creator/writer); "Pilot" (episode, writer); "Human Nature" (episode); "Still Life" (2005, TV Series, writer); "Angel" (1999, TV Series, writer); "She" (episode); *Just a Little Harmless*

Sex (1999); "Buffy the Vampire Slayer" (1997, TV Series, staff writer); "What's my Line?: Part 1" (episode, writer); [writer for episodes throughout:] "What's my Line?: Part 2" (episode); "Bad Eggs" (episode); "Surprise" (episode); "Bewitched, Bothered and Bewildered" (episode); "I Only Have Eyes for You" (episode); "Dead Man's Party" (episode); "Beauty and the Beasts" (episode); "Wish, The" (episode), "Consequences" (episode); "Prom, The" (episode); "Living Conditions" (episode); "Wild at Heart" (episode); "Doomed" (episode); "Goodbye Iowa" (episode); "New Moon Rising" (episode); "Buffy vs. Dracula" (episode); "Into the Woods" (episode); "Forever" (episode); "Bargaining: Part 1" (episode); "Wrecked" (episode); "Villains" (episode); "Bring On the Night" (episode).

KIM PEIRCE

Born in 1967 in Pennsylvania to teenage parents, she later attended the University of Chicago but dropped out because of financial difficulties. She worked in Japan, discovering photography, and came back to Chicago to finish her degree. After switching to film studies, Peirce went to graduate school at Columbia University's Film Department. She lives in New York.

Filmography: Boys Don't Cry (1999); *The Last Good Breath* (1998).

ANNA HAMILTON PHELAN

Raised in central Pennsylvania, she graduated from Emerson College in Boston in 1965 with a B.A. in theater arts. Phelan worked in the theater in Manhattan, and took time off to have a family before becoming a full-time screenwriter.

Filmography: Girl, Interrupted (1999); *Chains* (1999, aka Johnny Spain); *In Love and War* (1996, screenplay); *Gorillas in the Mist: The Story of Dian Fossey* (1988, screenplay/story); *Into the Homeland* (1987, TV); *Mask* (1985).

SALLY POTTER

Born Charlotte Sally Potter, September 19, 1949, in London, into an artistic family; her father was a designer and poet, her mother a musician. Both grandmothers were actresses. Potter attended schools in North London, decided to become a film director before age sixteen. She took a one-year course at St. Martin's School of Art in draughtsmanship and composition; between 1971 and 1974 Potter studied dance and choreography at the London School of Contemporary

Dance. She became a filmmaker's apprentice in the late 1960s at London Film-makers' Co-op.

Filmography: Yes (2004); *The Man Who Cried* (2000, also story); *The Tango Lesson* (1997); *Orlando* (1992); *The Gold Diggers* (1983); *London Story* (1980).

SUSAN RICE

Born in Michigan, and a graduate of Smith College, she earned a degree in philosophy, and a M.A. in literature from the University of Michigan. She has worked in Manhattan for the Motion Picture Association, Children's Film Theater, and Canadian film magazine *Take One.* Currently living in Manhattan, Rice keeps her 310 (CA) area code.

Filmography: When Andrew Came Home (2000, TV, aka *Taming Andrew,* UK); "The Lot" (1999, TV Series, writer); *A Match Made in Heaven* (1997, TV); *For Hope* (1996, TV); *Tears and Laughter: The Joan and Melissa Rivers Story* (1994, TV, aka *Starting Again*); *Opposites Attract* (1990, TV); *Animal Behavior* (1989); *Stamp of a Killer* (1987, TV, aka *Dangerous Affection*); *Something in Common* (1986, TV); *Enormous Changes at the Last Minute* (1983, aka *Enormous Changes*; aka *Trumps*).

MELISSA ROSENBERG

Born in Northern California, Rosenberg studied dance at Bennington College. Switching to the idea of a film career, she graduated from the Peter Stark Producing Program at the University of Southern California. She lives in Los Angeles.

Filmography: "The O.C." (2003, TV Series/teleplay); "Rescue, The" (episode, writer); "Outsider, The" (episode, writer); "Third Wheel, The" (episode, writer); "Birds of Prey" (2002, TV Series/teleplay); "Slick" (episode, writer); "Sins of the Mother" (episode, writer); "The Agency" (2001, TV Series); "The Magnificent Seven" (1998, TV Series); "Dark Skies" (1996, TV Series); "The Outer Limits" (1995, TV Series); "The Sentence" (episode); "Hercules: The Legendary Journeys" (1995, TV Series); "Party of Five" (1994, TV Series); "Class of '96" (1993, TV Series); "Dr. Quinn, Medicine Woman" (1993, TV Series); "If You Love Someone . . ." (episode); "One Touch of Nature" (episode); "Reunion" (episode).

PATRICIA ROZEMA

Born in 1958. Child of Dutch immigrants to Canada, she grew up in rural Ontario, and it did not see her first movie until she was sixteen. Raised in a strict Calvinist tradition, she now lives outside Toronto, and has one child.

Filmography: This Might Be Good (2000); *Mansfield Park* (1999); "The Hunger" (1997, TV Series); *Symposium: Ladder of Love* (1996, aka *Symposium*); *When Night Is Falling* (1995, aka *Quand tombe la nuit*, Canada: French title); *White Room* (1990); *I've Heard the Mermaids Singing* (1987); *Passion: A Letter in 16mm* (1985).

ALEXANDRA SEROS

This California native studied acting at the UCLA Theatre Arts Department. Seros is married, with one son, and lives in Santa Monica.

Filmography: The Specialist (1994); *Point of No Return* (1993).

ALLISON SILVERMAN

After graduating Phi Beta Kappa from Yale with a degree in humanities in 1994, she moved to Chicago to get work as an actress. Then she became a puppeteer and part of an improvisational comedy troupe traveling in Europe before returning to the United States. Silverman became a comedy writer: *Late Night with Conan O'Brien*, 1993–1996, and *The Daily Show* (Jon Stewart) 1996– .

Filmography: Late Night with Conan O'Brien: 10th Anniversary Special (2003, TV); "The Daily Show" (1996, TV Series); "Late Night with Conan O'Brien" (1993, TV Series).

ROBIN SWICORD

Born in Florida, she graduated from Florida State University. After working as a journalist in Florida, she moved to New York and supported herself as a copywriter; she wrote plays and had them mounted. After moving to California and becoming a successful screenwriter, Swicord married Nicholas Kazan, and is the mother of two girls.

Filmography: Memoirs of a Geisha (2005); *Practical Magic* (1998); *Matilda* (1996); *The Perez Family* (1995); *Little Women* (1994); *The Red Coat* (1993); *Shag* (1989, aka *Shag: The Movie*); *You Ruined My Life* (1987, TV); *Cuba Crossing* (1980, story/screenplay).

JOAN TEWKESBURY

Born April 3, 1936, in Redland, CA. Her mother was a nurse, her father worked for the Board of Education. After studying dance in New York and Los Angeles privately, she appeared on the New York stage (understudy for Mary Martin in *Peter Pan*), became a script girl for Robert Altman, then a writer-director on her own. Divorced with four grown children, Tewkesbury lives in Santa Monica, CA, and New Mexico.

Filmography: Scattering Dad (1998, teleplay); *Cold Sassy Tree* (1989, teleplay); *Elysian Fields* (1989, teleplay); *A Night in Heaven* (1983); *The Acorn People* (1981, teleplay); *The Tenth Month* (1979, teleplay); *Eyes of Laura Mars* (1978, uncredited); *Nashville* (1975); *Thieves Like Us* (1974).

EMMA THOMPSON

Born in London, April 15, 1959, she grew up in a theatrical household. She earned a degree in literature from Cambridge University. Her thesis was entitled: "George Eliot Had Failed to Create a True Female Hero." Married to and divorced from actor/director Kenneth Branagh, Thompson remarried and has one child.

Filmography: "Wit" (2001, teleplay); *Sense and Sensibility* (1995, screenplay); "Thompson" (1988, TV Series, writer); *An Evening for Nicaragua* (1983, TV); "Alfresco" (1983, TV Series, additional material); *Cambridge Footlights Revue* (1982, TV).

ROSE TROCHE

Troche grew up in the Chicago suburbs, part of a large Puerto Rican family. After making short films and videos, she enjoyed her feature film debut with the groundbreaking lesbian love story, *Go Fish*, premiered at Sundance Film; it won the "trophy award" there in 1994, and has become a cult classic. She lives in New York.

BARBARA TURNER

Born in Brooklyn, she studied acting at the University of Texas, and then returned to New York. She moved to California with actor-boyfriend Vic Morrow, whom she eventually married. Her acting career was supported by screenwriting work; and she eventually turned to screenwriting full-time. Divorced and remarried. Turner has three daughters, one of whom is actress Jennifer Jason Leigh, daughter of Morrow.

Filmography: The Company (2003, screenplay/story); *Pollock* (2000); *Beautiful*

View (2000); *Georgia* (1995); *Out of Darkness* (1994, TV); *Eye on the Sparrow* (1987, TV); *Sessions* (1983, TV); *Freedom* (1981, TV); *The War Between the Tates* (1977, TV); *The Dark Side of Innocence* (1976, TV, aka *The Hancocks*); *Widow* (1976, TV); *The Affair* (1973, TV); *Petulia* (1968, adaptation); *Deathwatch* (1966).

GINA WENDKOS

From Queens, NY, Wendkos studied painting at the Maryland Institute of Art, and received an M.A. degree at Hofberger School of Painting in 1978. She worked as a performance artist in Manhattan at La Mama, at the American Place Theater, and other venues, and was reviewed in the *New York Times* and the *Voice*. Positive reviews of her plays performed in California opened doors in television and film writing. She gave her age as twenty-six years old in 1982, thirty in 1985, and as her late thirties in 2003. Wendkos says that working as a bartender in New York, to support her career as a performance artist, was an experience that was helpful to her later in writing the film *Coyote Ugly*. Another aspect of her early years of struggle is that she once wrote copy for women answering telephones for "phone sex." Wendkos now lives in California, and is married with stepchildren.

Filmography: The Perfect Man (2005); *The Princess Diaries 2: Royal Engagement* (2004, story only); *The Princess Diaries* (2001); *Coyote Ugly* (2000); *Jersey Girl* (1992); "The Man in the Family" (1991, TV Series, writer); "Ginger Ale Afternoon" (1989, play); "Hooperman" (1987, TV Series, writer); "My Two Dads" (1987, TV Series, writer).

Notes

INTRODUCTION

1. MGM, under Irving Thalberg, had the best record for employing women writers throughout the 1930s and 1940s (though Warner Bros. was known during the war years for purposefully developing "women's films") and it showed in the success of the studio's movies. Anthony Slide writes in *Early Women Directors: Their Role in the Development of Silent Cinema*, "The caliber of these women [writers] stands out. They were writing some of the most memorable and important films of this period, including *Adam's Rib* (Ruth Gordon), *Anna Karenina* (Salka Viertel), *The Women* (Anita Loos), *Christopher Strong* (Zoë Akins), *Seven Brides for Seven Brothers*, *The Thin Man*, *Father of the Bride* (Frances Goodrich), *Singin' in the Rain* (Betty Comden)."

2. See Jeanine Basinger's *A Woman's View: How Hollywood Spoke to Women* (Knopf).

3. "Hollywood Dreams, Harsh Realities: Writing for Film and Television," *Contexts, the Magazine of the American Sociological Association* (Fall–Winter 2002). This way of looking at role models in media is a particularly American one. It is, loosely speaking, sociological. The assumption is that the images presented may both reflect and influence society. That approach really came to the fore in the 1970s with Molly Haskell's *From Reverence to Rape*. The other main critical tool is the structuralist method promoted by the British Film Institute and some of its acolytes: that a feminist interpretation of mainstream movies sometimes goes against the narrative line, and in traditional or patriarchal cinema depends upon "The Look"—to be deconstructed, often along semiotic lines.

CHAPTER ONE: GIVING MELODRAMA A GOOD NAME: THE FILM OF SENSIBILITY

1. Jeanine Basinger, *A Woman's View: How Hollywood Spoke to Women* (New York: Knopf, 1993).

2. Peter Biskind, *Down and Dirty Pictures: Miramax, Sundance, and the Rise of Independent Film* (Miramax Books, 2004).

CHAPTER TWO: VETS AND LIFERS: HOW THEY GOT AND STAYED IN

1. Linda Seger, *When Women Call the Shots* (New York: Henry Holt, 1996), 240, 254.

CHAPTER THREE: THE NEW PROFESSIONALS

1. Jason Gay, *New York Observer* (October 20, 2000).

2. Frances Marion, "She Wrote the Scripts of Some of the Milestone Movies," *Films in Review* 10, no. 3 (March 1969): 142.

CHAPTER FOUR: BREAKAWAY QUEENS AND GENRE BENDERS: WOMEN WRITERS STRETCHING AND BENDING THE FILM FORM

1. Marsha McCreadie, "Valuelessness and Vacillation in the Films of Julie Christie," *Journal of Popular Film* 6, no. 3 (1978): 216–228.

2. Suzanne Ferriss and Kathleen Waites, "Unclothing Gender: The Postmodern Sensibility in Sally Potter's *Orlando*," *Literature/Film Quarterly* 27 (1999): 110–115.

3. Sharon Willis, *High Contrast: Race and Gender in Contemporary American Film* (Durham, NC: Duke University Press, 1997), 108.

CHAPTER FIVE: ADAPTATION

1. Though George Eliot herself felt she had to compromise—due to letters and readers' demands in the serialized literary publication of her novel—and create an ending to her novel that was both storybook and sentimental.

2. Jane Austen, *Sense and Sensibility* (Baltimore: Penguin Books, 1969).

3. See Kay Jamison's *Touched with Fire: Manic-Depressive Illness and the Artistic Temperament* (New York: The Free Press, 1993).

CHAPTER SIX: THE INDEPENDENTS: FINDING A PERCH, HAVING THEIR SAY

1. Andrea Richards, *Girl Director: A How-to Guide for the First-Time Flat Broke Film Maker (and Video Maker)* (Los Angeles: Girl Press, 2001).

CHAPTER EIGHT: THE SMALLER SCREEN—TV: A BETTER FIT FOR WOMEN?

1. Dr. William T. Bielby and Dr. Denise D. Bielby, *The 1998 Hollywood Writers' Report: Telling All Our Stories* (Los Angeles: Writers Guild of America West).

2. Nora Ephron's interview is in Marsha McCreadie's *The Woman Who Write the Movies* (New York: Birch Lane Press, 1995).

3. *Slate* magazine, April 2001. Online.

CHAPTER NINE: THE VIEW FROM ABROAD

1. *Toronto Sun*. Clipping file in New Zealand File Commission office.

2. Interview by Douglas J. Rowe, Associated Press.

3. "Good Humor Gals," *Variety* (May 9–15, 2005).

CHAPTER TEN: CONCLUSION

1. Quoted in an article by Norman K. Dorn, *San Francisco Examiner* (December 5, 1976).

Selected Bibliography

Abramowitz, Rachel. *Is That a Gun in Your Pocket? Women's Experience of Power in Hollywood.* New York: Random House, 2000.

Basinger, Jeanine. *A Woman's View: How Hollywood Spoke to Women.* New York: Knopf, 1993.

Beauchamp, Cari. *Without Lying Down: Frances Marion and the Powerful Women of Early Hollywood.* New York: Scribners, 1997.

Bielby, Dr. William T., and Dr. Denise D. Bielby. *The 1998 Hollywood Writers' Report: Telling All Our Stories.* Los Angeles: Commissioned by Writers Guild of America West.

Biskind, Peter. *Down and Dirty Pictures: Miramax, Sundance, and the Rise of Independent Film.* New York: Simon & Schuster, 2004.

Burton, Julianne, and Suzanna Pick. "The Women Behind the Camera." *Heresies* 16 (1983): 46–50.

Carroll, Noel. "The Image of Women in Film: A Defense of a Paradigm." *The Journal of Aesthetics and Art Criticism* 48 (Fall 1990): 349–360.

Doan, Mary Ann, Patricia Mellancamp, and Linda Williams. *Re-Vision: Essays in Feminist Film Criticism.* Washington, DC: American Film Institutes, 1984.

Ehrenreich, Barbara. *Nickel and Dimed: On (Not) Getting by in America.* New York: Metropolitan Books, 2001.

Ferriss, Suzanne, and Kathleen Waites. "Unclothing Gender: The Postmodern Sensibility in Sally Potter's *Orlando*." *Literature/Film Quarterly* 27 (1999): 110–115.

Foster, Gwendolyn Audrey. *Women Film Directors: An International Bio-Critical Dictionary.* Westport, CT: Greenwood Press, 1995.

Gillet, Sue. "Angel from the Mirror City: Jane Campion's Janet Frame." www.sensesofcinema.com.

Gilligan, Carol. *In a Different Voice: Psychological Theory and Women's Development*. Cambridge, MA, and London: Harvard University Press, 1982.

Grant, Susanna. *Erin Brockovich*. New York: Newmarket Press, 2000.

Gregory, Mollie. *Women Who Run the Show*. New York: St. Martin's Press, 2002.

Haskell, Molly. *From Reverence to Rape*. Chicago: University of Chicago Press, 1977.

Jamison, Kay. *Touched with Fire: Manic-Depressive Illness and the Artistic Temperament*. New York: The Free Press, 1993.

Klainberg, Lesli. *In the Company of Women*. Documentary about independent women filmmakers. 2004.

Kuhn, Annette. *Women's Pictures: Feminism and the Cinema*. 2nd ed. London and New York: Verso, 1994.

Kuhn, Annette, with Susannah Radstone. *Women in Film: An International Guide*. New York: Fawcett Columbine, 1990.

Lefcourt, Peter, and Laura J. Shapiro, eds. *The First Time I Got Paid for It: Writer's Tales from the Hollywood Trenches*. New York: Public Affairs, 2000.

Mayne, Judith. "Feminist Film Theory and Criticism." *Signs* 11, no. 1 (Autumn, 1985): 81–100.

————. *The Woman at the Keyhole: Feminism and Women's Cinema*. Bloomington: Indiana University Press, 1990.

McCreadie, Marsha. "Valuelessness and Vacillation in the Films of Julie Christie." *The Journal of Popular Film* 6, no. 3 (1978): 216–228.

————. *The Women Who Write the Movies*. New York: Birch Lane Press, 1995.

McFarlane, Brain, Geoff Mayer, and Ina Bertrand, eds. *The Oxford Companion to Australian Film*. New York: Oxford University Press, 1999.

McGilligan, Patrick. *Backstory: Interviews with Screenwriters of Hollywood's Golden Age*. Berkeley, CA: University of California Press.

Mulvey, Laura. *Screen* 16, no 3 (Autumn 1975): 6–18.

Parill, Sue. *Jane Austen on Film and Television: A Critical Study of the Adaptations*. Jefferson, NC: McFarland & Co., 2002.

Phillips, Julia. *You'll Never Eat Lunch in This Town Again*. New York: Random House, 1991.

Richards, Andrea. *Girl Director: A How-to Guide for the First-Time Flat Broke Film Maker (and Video Maker)*. Forward by Allison Anders. Los Angeles: Girl Press, 2001.

Schwartz, Nancy Lynn. *The Hollywood Writers' Wars*. New York: Alfred A. Knopf, 1982.

Seger, Linda. *When Women Call the Shots*. New York: Henry Holt, 1996.

Shlain, Leonard. *The Alphabet Versus the Goddess*. New York: Penguin, 2004.

Slide, Anthony. *Early Women Directors: Their Role in the Development of the Silent Cinema.* New York: A. S. Barnes, 1977.

Wexman, Virginia Wright. *Jane Campion: Interviews.* Jackson: University Press of Mississippi, 1999.

Whitmont, Edward C. *Return of the Goddess.* New York: Crossroad, 1992.

Willis, Sharon. *High Contrast: Race and Gender in Contemporary Hollywood Film.* Durham, NC: Duke University Press, 1997.

Women Make Movies. Catalogue. New York: Women Make Movies Inc., 1994.

Index

About the Author

MARSHA McCREADIE has written about women and film throughout her career as a professor at Rutgers University and as a film critic at the *Arizona Republic*. She has published numerous reviews and essays for such publications as *Films in Review*, *American Film*, *Premiere*, the *New York Times*, and the *Los Angeles Times*, and is the author of three books on women and film, one of which, *Women on Film: The Critical Eye*, won the Dartmouth College Award for Best Dramatic Criticism and the *Choice* Outstanding Book Award in 1983.